COUSTEAU'S
GREAT
WHITE
SHARK

JEAN-MICHEL COUSTEAU AND MOSE RICHARDS

HARRY N. ABRAMS, INC.

PUBLISHERS, NEW YORK

COUSTEAU'S
GREAT
WHITE
SHARK

Editor: Robert Morton
Designer: Bob McKee
Photo Editor: Judy K. Brody
Scientific Consultants: Dr. Richard C. Murphy
and Wesley R. Strong, Jr.
Publications Coordinator: Lesley D. High

*The Cousteau Society wishes to thank the Turner
Broadcasting System and Amaya Films, whose support
made possible the expedition chronicled in this book.*

Library of Congress Cataloging-in-Publication Data
Cousteau, Jean-Michel.
   *Cousteau's great white shark / Jean-Michel Cousteau
and Mose Richards.*
      p.   cm.
   Includes index.
   ISBN 0–8109–3181–8
   1. White shark—Queensland—Great Barrier Reef.
I. Richards, Mose.
QL638.95.L3C68   1992
˙597'.31—dc20   92–7983
                                         CIP

Printed and bound in Italy

*The Cousteau Society is a nonprofit membership-
supported organization dedicated to the protection and
improvement of the quality of life for present and future
generations.*

The Cousteau Society
870 Greenbrier Circle, Suite 402
Chesapeake, VA 23320

CONTENTS

ACKNOWLEDGMENTS

We would like to thank especially chief diver Steve Arrington, whose detailed and lively journals helped us recount these expeditions, and Wesley R. (Rocky) Strong, Jr., whose scientific direction and interpretation not only helped translate our field work into professional treatises, but into a film and this book as well. Thanks to Barry Bruce and the South Australian Department of Fisheries and the crew of the R.V. *Ngerin* for their partnership in gathering the vital and new information included herein, and to our colleague Dr. Richard C. Murphy, who helped guide the planning of the expeditions and offered thoughtful suggestions about this manuscript.

We are deeply indebted to Rodney Fox and to Valerie and Ron Taylor, who not only gave freely their advice borne of many years related experience, but also of their time and their philosophical support "on behalf of the great white shark," as Valerie put it. We are grateful to Bob Talbot for his generous contributions of time and talent, and to Chuck Davis, who often took on the taxing roles of both still photographer and cinematographer on several expeditions.

Kind thanks also to the National Parks and Wildlife Service of South Australia for permission to conduct research at Dangerous Reef, and to Ocean Technology Systems and the California Department of Fish and Game for lending us some essential equipment. Shark specialists Dr. Don Nelson and Dr. John Stevens graciously contributed their time to our expeditions, and we are both grateful and honored by their involvement.

Finally, we would like to acknowledge the behind-the-scenes assistance of Yehuda Goldman, who does not appear in the film documenting our expeditions nor in this account, but whose logistical magic and full-time devotion were instrumental in bringing the project to a successful conclusion.

ONE THE MOST FRIGHTENING ANIMAL ON EARTH

*It has rightfully been
called a top carnivore,
a killing machine,
the last free predator of
man—the most frightening
animal on earth.*
EDWARD O. WILSON

The moon casts a white slick across the sea, which is furrowed tonight. The light breaks on the swells and scatters like bobbing torches. Probably *she* is aware of the full moon, too, as she glides. She cannot comprehend the moon's nature, but perhaps she uses the neon glow it casts down through the black waters, as we in our world use streetlights.

We are above her by the height of a mature hardwood tree. It is as if she were wandering a nighttime meadow, and we were tracking her surreptitiously from a blimp above. She is probably aware of the blue tube on her back. Two flat thumbnail-sized steel barbs keep it there. A light pole-spear wielded by scientist Rocky Strong set it in place as she passed a yard from *Alcyone*'s swim step, where he stood. The barbs are designed to minimize pain, but if she perceives merely that something is causing a drag, or producing a dull sensation along her raspy skin, she may surmise that a remora has attached itself to her like a flea to a lion.

She may hear the pinging calls emitted from the tube and sense the electromagnetic field it produces, but she is unlikely to know that we are following the device through the night, tracing her movements through the three dimensions of her liquid realm, curious to know her path. No one in the world knows where she or her kind spend most of their time. No one really knows much at all about her species. This is curious, since there is no creature on earth we humans fear more or love

With her prominent snout pierc-
ing the waters aft of Alcyone, *this*
ten-footer—nicknamed Clarabell
by the Cousteau team—amply
illustrates why Australians call the
species white pointers .Under-
sides are universally white,
perhaps prompting early sailors to
call them "great whites." Though
dorsal color patterns vary
considerably, backs are generally
dark, gradually turning from dun
grey to slate grey as the sharks
mature.

to fear so consummately. Pronounce the words "great white" and the subject is unquestioned. The wide-eyed child will know what you are talking about, and so will the panicked snorkeler.

On the bridge, navigator Pascal Pique is giving linear form to our great white's path this night, pencilling a zigzag line across a nautical chart. The line represents the shark's meanderings since 8:30 last evening, and it will continue across the chart until the blue tube pulls away from the shark's skin and sinks to the bottom, or until interference, weather, or error causes us to lose her.

The first such tracking was of a shark dubbed *Chris* by *Alcyone*'s crew, after their captain, Christophe Jouet-Pastre. The chase lasted thirteen hours before an odd intervention brought it to an end. A pack of dolphins became intrigued by the pings and arrived to investigate. Perhaps this alien sound in their waters was akin to a UFO in our skies. They seemed captivated, even rhapsodic. Eventually, they closed to within a foot of the team's underwater hydrophone receiver and shrieked into it so loudly that biologist Barry Bruce ripped off the headphones in pain.

This is the fourth tracking. Pascal works alone etching the route beneath a single reading light. The tracking record is one of the duties of his watch. Along the top of the chart, a crewman has recorded earlier the name of the living question mark sliding below, a brain-guided missile of flesh that turns, ascends, descends, hovers, darts for reasons we can only guess. We know she is female but little more. We cannot know her purposes beyond the obvious ones of plucking food from the waters and procreating. We cannot know if she turned eastward suddenly because of a scent or a sound or a sensed movement or a perceived electrical field. Or a mere whim. Perhaps she is an aberrant individual, a little crazy. There are maniacs in our human world, why not in the populations of other species? Perhaps she is a model representative of her kindred great whites in every way.

We know only her rough trajectory across about twenty-seven hours, and we know that she approached us uneasily from the beginning, lunging for our bait after hours of passing us in wary observation. Imputing to her a strain of independence—anathema to science but a diversion during long hours at sea—an inspired crewman nicknamed her *Murf*, after Cousteau Society chief scientist Dr. Richard C. Murphy, a born diver who would cruise the depths far from civilization and seldom return if he were blessed with gills.

At the time, the shark was believed to be a male, but during the implanting of the telemetry transmitter her lack of claspers near the anal fin became obvious. *Murf* was a female. And

for the amused crew this further added to the drollness of having named a white shark after their chief scientist.

We are off the southern coast of Australia, eighteen nautical miles out of Port Lincoln along a barren hump of rock called Dangerous Reef. Featureless but for the birds and sea lions that swarm to it, the tiny island would seem of little interest were it not for the ocean creatures that seem to congregate along its underwater flanks. For great white sharks, the sea-grass bottom and the water column encircling Dangerous Reef seem to be a kind of Place de l'Etoile, a kind of Grand Central Station. Those who would study or film these infamous predators come here, as we on the Cousteau team have come aboard the windship *Alcyone*.

I have dreamed of such an expedition since boyhood. While that may not be an uncommon fantasy among young people craving exotic adventure, I had a special interest. My father and his friends had seen a great white shark, had actually dived with one. JYC (pronounced "*Zheek*," a nickname coined by family and friends from *Jacques-Yves Cousteau*) wrote of the incident in his best-selling book *The Silent World*, published in 1953.

During an encounter with a shark in the Cape Verde Islands, at a distance of 40 feet there appeared from the grey haze the lead-white bulk of a 25-foot Carcharodon carcharias, *the only shark species that all specialists agree is a confirmed man-eater. Dumas, my bodyguard, closed in beside me. The brute was swimming lazily. Then the shark saw us. His reaction was the least conceivable one. In pure fright, the monster voided a cloud of excrement and departed at an incredible speed.*

Today, JYC probably would describe such an encounter differently. His estimate of size likely was exaggerated by the refractive power of water, since no white shark has yet been reliably measured longer than nineteen-and-a-half feet. And years of personal rapport with undersea life have deleted from his vocabulary such words as brute and monster when describing marine creatures. Yet his momentary glimpse of a great white prompted the question that lingered for decades in my mind and has brought us to South Australia today: while we know from record books that the white shark is capable of killing humans, is it truly the devious murderer portrayed commonly in popular literature and films? If so, why would the unchallenged lord of the sea bolt so timidly at the sight of divers huddling together defensively? I recall that the lesson drawn by my father was that one could never tell what a shark might do. That has been a guiding principle in our work aboard *Calypso* and *Alcyone*. Unless our goal is to film and observe sharks, we

Largest carnivorous fish in the sea, and most feared of all sharks, the great white is found in all oceans, but is most abundant along the cool, temperate coasts of North America, South Africa, and Western and South Australia.

stay out of their way whenever possible, leaving the water to avoid any dangerous confrontations. It is their realm, not ours.

The opportunity to understand more about white sharks came during a major two-year expedition in Australia. While Cousteau Society land teams explored the interior of the continent and our vessels sailed completely around the coast, I learned of a movement among local conservation groups to add the white shark to Australia's Threatened Species List. According to many divers, fishermen, tour boat operators and others, the number of great whites sighted along the coast of South Australia seems to be declining year by year. Historically, these waters are renowned for white sharks. When producers of such movies as *Blue Water, White Death* and *Jaws* needed live-action scenes of whites, their production crews came to the constellation of tiny islands at the mouth of Spencer Gulf. When sportfishermen sought to capture record-breaking whites, they often came to these same waters.

The population of great whites along southern Australia may

not be the world's largest. The species is found elsewhere, especially along the west and east coasts of the United States and South Africa. But these whites had traditionally been the most accessible and scientists believed it possible one day to delve into the true nature of the creatures here. If whites were disappearing from southern Australia, so was the best opportunity to study them.

Yet when the Australian Threatened Fishes Committee met in Townsville in 1989 to consider a recommendation to protect

The Cousteau windship Alcyone *served as research base for the study and filming of great white sharks on four expeditions during two years off the South Australia coast. The vessel's two Turbosail cylinders—developed by an engineering team led by Jacques-Yves Cousteau—act as hollow wings, creating an air-pressure difference that "pulls" the ship forward with four to five times the efficiency of traditional fabric sails.*

the species, the proposal was rejected. The decision was not based on any evidence that the whites were a robust population but on the dearth of information about the species. There simply was not enough known about great whites to determine their status. There was no way to gauge reliably if whites were declining in number, no way to identify the cause of their demise if such was the case.

The South Australian Department of Fisheries quickly organized a research program to collect new data on the sharks and to analyze carefully the sketchy information contained in past reports of sightings and captures. But they did not have the resources to investigate living sharks in the wild. Their information would have to come from white sharks observed by sailors, or caught by fishermen. Our presence in the area was fortuitous. We had an efficient vessel nearby and available—*Alcyone*—from which to mount a study of great whites. We had a crew of experienced sailors, divers, scientists and filmmakers aboard. We had financial backing for such an endeavor from American Ted Turner and his television network, TBS. And, most importantly, we had long awaited such an opportunity. We were lucky enough to meet Barry Bruce, the young senior researcher in charge of the Department of Fisheries white shark program and he was enthusiastic about collaborating with us. Working with Fisheries, we outlined a series of both scientific and cinematic experiments that comprised the longest and most ambitious white shark expedition in history. My lifelong dream was about to come true.

It is one thing to make an objective decision to study an animal cloaked in mystery and myth. It is another to contemplate the realities of diving with a predator large enough and powerful enough to end a human life almost instantaneously. Few divers have as much experience in the sea as our teams and we know from half a century of exploration that we have more to fear from our own errors in the ocean than from the creatures who inhabit it.

Yet we are human. Stories of the savagery associated with sharks have been stored indelibly in our memories. An awareness that few sharks are truly dangerous does not always inhibit a rise in the heart rate when we catch sight unexpectedly of that notorious shape in the distant haze. Now, we would be mingling underwater with the ultimate shark, the supershark. We would take every precaution, but we were not necessarily

Alcyone anchors near Dangerous Reef. Though the name of the tiny island was bestowed by early sailors to mark it as a navigational hazard, the reef has become notorious as a gathering place for great white sharks, which seem drawn to its underwater flanks.

certain what precautions to take, what the capabilities and behavior of this vaunted hunter might be.

We had to confront our own deep feelings. Doing so, I was led to speculate on the irrational fears that color our perception of sharks in general. For the dread we feel toward the great white shark is just an intensification of the human fear of all sharks.

Why sharks? There are other fierce animals on earth. One answer might be that the other potential predators of humanity have almost uniformly been extinguished, tamed, or banished beyond easy contact by industrialized society. The sabre-toothed tiger is gone. The African lion is corralled by game-reserve boundaries. The grizzly bear survives only in the faraway north country. The timber wolf paces nervously along zoo fences. In many parts of the tropics, the crocodile is routinely raised in farm ponds, as sequestered as a chicken in a poultry shed.

We have grown comfortable, even protective, of the other beasts capable of devouring us whole, but for one. We are the masters of virtually every biological tract of earth, but for one. We remain potential food for creatures patrolling the liquid wilds encircling our terrestrial kingdoms. We enter the sea knowingly at the mercy of the last animal still beyond our dominion. The very word by which we call the creature evokes an inner shudder, awakens a dark genetic anxiety as old as life itself. As biologists Samuel Gruber and Charles Manire point out, the English word *shark* is derived from a middle English word, *shurke*, which was purely derogatory and the hatred it expressed centuries ago is continued in such expressions as *loan shark* and *pool shark*.

Our good friend Valerie Taylor, who was to join us on the expedition and who has spent a great deal of her life swimming with sharks, tells the story of a survey conducted in the late 1960s in Australia to determine which single word had the greatest psychological impact on people. Researchers tested the reactions to words like rape, death, murder, sex, love, spider, poison, snake. Among every conceivable word associated with danger or passion, it was the word *shark* that elicited the most emotional response among the people surveyed.

It is easy to understand the basic fear of sharks, but why such an irrational, vehement fear of them?

The randomness, for one thing. Any swimmer can suddenly disappear in the sea beneath a cloud of blood, punctured and torn by a mouth at the end of a living gray rocket. Or so it seems.

The lack of warning, as well. There is no way to scan the undersea vista to be certain that all is clear of sharks. In the sea we are ever aware that a shark *could* be heading directly toward us. We know it is always unlikely but we also know it is always possible.

The furious violence associated with them, of course. The words "feeding frenzy" evoke images of chaotic murder in the minds of most of us. We imagine surviving a plane crash at sea only to be devoured horribly by maniacal sharks in a froth of churning, blood-stained water. We imagine that feeding frenzies occur commonly, although they are rarely witnessed and most of those documented have been induced for scientific or moviemaking purposes.

There is the silence of the shark, too. Unlike most large creatures, the shark has no organ with which to produce sound. Many other fish can make primitive sounds using their swim bladders, but the shark has none. Sharks do not roar or bellow or bark. Moreover, the denticles—or scales—along the bodies of many sharks are hydrodynamically designed to diminish the sound of the animals swimming. They are truly "silent" swimmers, and perhaps this soundless aspect of sharks equates in the human mind with stealth.

Many sharks, like the great white, also seem to travel alone for the most part and are thereby cast in a role that is disconcerting to human society, that of the "loner." Unlike marine mammals, sharks do not inspire us to attribute to them admirable human traits of warmth, humor, play, or parental concern. There is no obvious reason to love sharks. In fact, even many animal-protection supporters probably would accept the age-old dictum that "the only good shark is a dead shark."

And, finally, there is the cold efficiency that attends to their feeding. Our ancestors may have feared other carnivores with teeth-laden jaws, but today we assume that only sharks lurk in proximity to us with the strength, opportunity, or ambition to gather meat at will from a living human being.

They do not do so often. The frequency of their attacks on people make them an insignificant threat to us statistically. The list of dangers more likely to result in human death than shark attacks includes mosquitos, bees, dogs, pigs, lightning, even tramplings by elephants. More people die in bathtubs and backyard swimming pools than die from shark bites in the sea.

The most accepted estimate of fatalities from shark attacks comes from the International Shark Attack File, which was initiated in 1957 by Leonard P. Schultz and Perry Gilbert. During ten years of research Schultz and his staff at the Smithsonian Institution assembled information on shark attacks dating as far back as 1580, when a sailor was attacked after falling overboard on a voyage from Portugal to India. U. S. naval officer David Baldridge took these historical records and

*Jean-Michel Cousteau finalizes
expedition plans with principal
team members in* Alcyone's *carré
(crew lounge). From the left are:
chief diver Steve Arrington,
engineer Paul Martin, diver
Capkin Van Alphen, Cousteau,
chief cinematographer Michel
Deloire, and assistant cameraman
Antoine Rosset.*

OVERLEAF:
*Cousteau divers await great white
sharks during a 1986 voyage to
the Farallon Islands, west of San
Francisco, California. Though
whites are known to frequent the
area, the team sighted none
despite days of baiting.*

analyzed them by computer, eliminating those in which the information seemed unreliable. In 1973 he published a report based on a total of 1,165 attacks. From his work, Schultz and Gilbert concluded that there were 30 to 50 recorded attacks per year on humans, with the caveat that some no doubt go unrecorded in the developing world. Of these, they believe not more than 25 to 30 are fatal. Today, most researchers round the figure off to 25 per year. As Gruber and Manire point out, a single air disaster would cover a decade of shark attacks and one month's auto accidents result in more deaths than the entire recorded history of shark attacks.

In the case of attacks by great whites, easily the most feared of all sharks, there are no worldwide figures available, but what we do know suggests that such incidents are extremely rare. Along the western coast of the United States, there may be less than one per year, and the same appears to be true in southern Australia.

In fact, the great white itself seems a rare creature in the ocean. During all my years of diving, often in waters known to be inhabited by white sharks, I had never once sighted a great white underwater until we undertook extraordinary efforts to attract them during the present expedition. In 1986, *Alcyone* visited the Farallon Islands off San Francisco, part of a cold-water region believed to support one of the world's largest white shark populations. We were equipped with cameras and an antishark cage, and we baited for whites, but we did not see even a single dorsal fin.

OPPOSITE:
When gallons of fish and animal blood failed to lure great whites during the Farallon expedition, the Cousteau team began to question the abundance of sharks in the area. Speculation about declining great white numbers led them eventually to South Australia, where they mounted the most ambitious white shark expedition in history.

ABOVE:
Sometimes reaching a length of sixty feet, the whale shark—Rhiniodon typus—is not only the largest of all sharks but the largest fish in the sea. Though fearsome in appearance and about three times the size of adult great whites, the plankton-eater poses no danger to human swimmers.

Further evidence for the scarcity of great whites comes from commercial fishing records. Between Cape Hatteras and Cape Cod, another area known for great whites, longline fishermen took a total of 4,770 sharks in the years 1961 to 1967. Only 36 were great white sharks.

In general, of about 350 known species of sharks, most pose no danger whatsoever to humans. They range in size from the foot-long dwarf shark (*Squaliolus laticaudus*), to the whale shark (*Rhincodon typus*), which can reach a length of sixty feet and a weight of more than ten tons. The largest fish in the sea, the whale shark behaves much like its baleen namesakes, swimming torpidly along the surface, harmlessly straining plankton and small fishes through its delicate gill rakers. And though most sharks are efficient hunters, few attain a size much larger than about four feet. Many live a rather sluggish existence along the sea floor and would no more consider attacking a human swimmer than we might contemplate biting a Doberman.

Yet that image etched in our minds by Winslow Homer and Ernest Hemingway and Steven Spielberg is so sensational that it overrides reason when most of us step or dive into the sea, and a mild queasiness lingers in many of us until we leave the water. It is neither panic nor terror. It is the discomfort of being at the mercy of another being, for most of us an insecurity worse even than the fear of flying, since a member of our own species is in the cockpit of an airplane, guided by a brain that is probably capable of killing us through error but not hunger.

Our instinct compels us to eliminate threats, and so we might envision a sea cleansed of danger. If there were no sharks the ocean would be more like an endless swimming pool, we imagine. But it would not be the ocean, not the real ocean, not

Nearly depleted by spearfishing and mesh-net captures, Australia's grey nurse sharks, Eugomphodus taurus, *are now safeguarded by the government of New South Wales, the first shark species in the world accorded such protection. Recently, as a result of relentless pressure by fishermen seeking their jaws to sell as souvenirs, great whites of South Africa became the second protected shark species.*

the ocean shaped by sharks as sharks have been shaped by the ocean, not the ocean kept biologically sleek and dynamic by sharks scouring away the ill and the malformed and the decrepit, not the real ocean anymore than Van Gogh would be the real Van Gogh without yellow.

As it happens, sharks dwell in the darkness, beyond and beneath our horizon of life. They fly through an opaque sky so foreign as to be composed of a different state of matter than the air enveloping us. We cannot easily nor for long periods enter the world where sharks live and breathe, find nourishment, mate, give birth, and die. We cannot observe them through binoculars while nibbling from a picnic basket. They roam the dim seas of our imagination, symbols of the terrible unknown to human minds still tainted by prehistoric impulses.

But the genius of humanity is to explore, to open the mysteries and peer inside, to see how things work, to illuminate darkness. It is time to turn our curiosity and not our vengeance upon our last mythic animal enemy. The solution to our dread is not to eliminate sharks but to understand them. To our great surprise we may find that, of all things, we want to protect the great white shark.

As our team aboard *Alcyone* began poring over available white shark information sent to us by Barry Bruce and our own Cousteau Society scientists Dick Murphy and Rocky Strong, we were astounded by the number of basic facts regarding the life of white sharks that remain unknown to science.

While there are bits and pieces of information provided by captures, by stomach analyses, by attacks, by brief studies—all of which have led to a great deal of speculation—there are great gaps in our proven knowledge of white sharks.

Consider the following. We do not have even a remote idea how many exist in the world, or how many there are locally in confirmed ranges, and whether they are on the increase or decrease. We do not know how closely white sharks around the world are related. We do not know exactly where they live. We do not know if they are nomads or seasonal migrants. We do not know how deep they go, or if their vertical range changes by day and night or by season. We do not know if they generally live alone or in pairs or if there is anything approaching social relationships among them. We do not know if the sexes live apart. We do not know how long they live. We do not know where they breed, how often, or how many young they produce. We do not know precisely how often they need to eat, what their preferred prey is, or whether they depend on different food sources in different parts of the world. We do not know what interest they have in eating humans. We do not know with certainty what attracts them to prey, or which of their senses might be most valuable in detecting food. We do not know how "smart" they may be, or how "vicious." We do not even know for certain how large they get.

One of the reasons for this paucity of information is that, unlike some other shark species, great whites have never been kept and observed successfully in captivity. More than a dozen attempts have failed. At Marineland in Florida, a white died thirty-five hours after capture. At San Francisco's Steinhart Aquarium, a great white lived for three-and-a-half days, but became so disoriented in a display tank that it was released.

What we *do* know about great white sharks is largely historical, anatomical, and anecdotal.

on the planet is testament not to primordial savagery but to extraordinary fitness.

As sharks go, however, the great white is a rather new model, perhaps appearing only about four million years ago. It is widely associated with the extinct giant called *Carcharodon megalodon*, which lived about sixty million years ago. Its estimated length of forty feet has been calculated from six-inch-high fossil teeth. Since the teeth appear almost identical in shape to those of the modern white shark, it is assumed that whites are either direct descendants of *C. megalodon* or that the two had a common ancestor.

Whatever secret evolutionary saga led to the great whites we see today, it could serve as a manual for development of natural

Cousteau Society biologist Rocky Strong measures the teeth of a great white captured by a South Australian fisherman. The team found the shark's head frozen and preserved in a meat locker.

Scientists have discovered that the enamel height of shark teeth corresponds roughly with the creature's total length, enabling specialists to estimate size based on a shark's largest tooth.

tools of aggression. Navy man David Baldridge, who analyzed the International Shark Attack File, has described the white shark as an "integrated weapons system." First and foremost, that's what we know beyond doubt about the great white shark—it is supremely equipped to hunt in the sea and to consume whatever it pleases.

To begin with, sharks have superb and multifaceted detection systems for locating prey. The image that comes to mind is the marine-animal equivalent of a modern fighter jet seeking targets with a high-tech instrumentation package invented by nature.

Some researchers believe that sound may be the most important shark sense for hunting. They probably hear low-frequency vibrations, such as those emitted by struggling or wounded fish, at distances greater than a mile. Complementary to the information gathered by their inner ears is a lateral-line

The first sharklike fish swam through Devonian seas dominated by large armored fishes some four hundred million years ago. Sharks have therefore been around more than a hundred times longer, in Harvard biologist Edward Wilson's phrase, than "anything that could remotely be called human." The antiquity of the species has led to a misconception that sharks are primitive. In fact, evolution has gradually fashioned a highly sophisticated creature in the shark, and its long duration system like those of most fish, in which vibrations, pressure changes and waves, and movements of water are detected by a series of sensory canals extending along the sides of the head and body.

The shark sense of smell is so keen that the creatures have been called swimming noses. They have the ability to scent food over great distances in the water, and it is generally accepted that sharks can detect blood in concentrations as small as one part of blood per million parts of sea water.

Not a great deal is known about the sense of taste in sharks, but it is believed to be important. There are taste buds in their mouths (even some scattered over the surfaces of their bodies), and some researchers speculate that their attacks on humans

what they track down. Tremendous musculature arranged in a sleek, hydrodynamic body gives many sharks the ability to overcome prey with speed and strength. With a maximum weight estimated at between 5,000 and 7,000 pounds, a great white can bring to bear on its victims a bodily mass equivalent to the weight of a couple of small cars.

And then there are the teeth.

Despite Peter Benchley's infamous title, it is probably the teeth of a shark that prompt our anxieties more than its jaws. Like other sharks, great whites are armed with bladelike teeth arrayed in rows about its mouth. Whenever front teeth are lost during feeding, the waiting replacements move forward as if on a conveyor belt. But the teeth of the white may be the most

may often be test bites to gather information about an unusual object simply by tasting a sample of it.

It was long believed that sharks had poor vision, but recent studies suggest their eyes are highly developed and designed much like those of terrestrial vertebrates. And if that were not enough hunting equipment, sharks have a detection system that is unique and is one of the most remarkable in all nature. This actual sixth sense enables them to find prey by picking up weak electric fields, such as those generated by all living things. It means that a shark can probably locate prey even buried under sand on the sea floor. Some researchers believe this sense may act as an accurate internal electromagnetic compass, enabling sharks to navigate by the earth's magnetic field.

The extraordinary senses that allow sharks to find food are matched by awesome physical gear for catching and eating

The Cousteau team discovered this fossil shark tooth embedded in a cliff near Exmouth, Western Australia. After excavating and examining the tooth, they reburied it and alerted National Park authorities. An Australian dollar—about the size of an American quarter—provides a sense of scale. The team concluded that the tooth came from a shark almost certainly ancestral to the great white.

formidable of any shark. They are large, triangular, and serrated, enabling the creature not only to bite with great efficiency but effectively to saw away the meat it seeks. It is as if nature outfitted the animal with a huge maw studded with wedgelike steak knives.

It is not hard to understand why sharks in general, and great whites in particular, have been called near-perfect killing machines. Yet the known traits of the white shark constitute

In Alcyone's radio room, Jean-Michel Cousteau and ship's captain Nicolas Dourassoff, right, monitor the dive team's encounters with great whites. The control panel enables Dourassoff to manipulate an undersea video camera and to steer the ROV— Remotely Operated Vehicle—to which it is mounted.

OPPOSITE TOP:
Divers return to Alcyone's rear deck in one of two metal shark cages employed during the expeditions. After studying existing cages, the Cousteau team designed and built new models. Wide camera ports and the lack of corner supports enhance camera maneuverability, and stainless-steel materials emanate a weaker electrical field than galvanized steel—causing less impact on shark behavior.

only the physical beast. To really understand the white shark we will have to learn the spectrum of its behavior. Our quest in the coming expedition was twofold. One, to assess the nature of the animal and determine whether its reputation, its popular image as an "evil" force, is justified. We would do so by developing a series of experiments, by observing the animals over an extended period, and by filming their behavior whenever possible to provide both scientists and the public with a more complete view of an animal seldom observed in the wild. And two, we would help the South Australian Fisheries Department initiate a scientific study that will one day enable researchers to determine its status.

Barry Bruce estimates that it may take twenty years to know if South Australia's great whites are in decline. We could not therefore establish proof one way or another during our expedition, but we could set in motion the collection of data for future analysis. In order to determine the best management policies for a species like the great white, one must know the size, movements, and rate of replacement of the population. We would organize the largest operation ever attempted to tag and track white sharks.

While Barry worked with Rocky Strong and Dick Murphy to devise the scientific aspects of our expedition, I set about organizing the logistics. What we anticipated as a single voyage covering a few weeks and carried out by Alcyone's crew of twelve would eventually expand to five voyages during nearly three years, involving a total of forty people. Joining us would be some of the foremost shark specialists in the world, as well as divers and photographers with decades of shark experience.

Alcyone's captain, Nicolas Dourassoff (who would guide the vessel during two of the five trips, and would be replaced by Christophe Jouet-Pastre when called to other duties) began studying charts of our intended research area in lower Spencer Gulf with navigator Thierry Stern. I directed *Alcyone*'s chief diver Steve Arrington to assemble the special equipment needed for filming whites underwater. Initially we rented two antishark cages, but design limitations in them led us to build our own. Improvements were conceived by Dourassoff and our veteran engineers Paul Martin and Joe Cramer. The new stainless-steel cages, constructed by Cramer, represent a state-of-the-art design. I envisioned a new kind of protective cage as well, one employing the clear plastic called LEXAN, a material so strong that it is used in the bulletproof windows of presidential limousines. Work was begun to design and build a one-man cylindrical cage of this plastic, which we hoped would appear nearly invisible in the sea and offer the opportunity to conduct several new kinds of experiments.

Louis Prezelin, who has accompanied us on worldwide expeditions over some twenty-five years, would be the first chief cinematographer for the expedition, aided by American cameraman Chuck Davis and our diver-assistant cameraman Antoine Rosset. With the addition of Australian diver Capkin Van Alphen, sound engineer Mike Westgate, and our chef Bruno Gicquel, who doubles as a deckhand and diver, we were ready to set out in search of whites. Our team represented four nations and a multitude of disciplines, all bound together by such a compelling, shared fascination with the sea that they willingly endure the travails and the deprivations of long periods at sea with us. Our films highlight the adventure of Cousteau Society work romantically colored by symphonic music, but the reality of our expeditions often entails a great deal more drudgery and boredom than exhilaration. Few missions, however, have involved the potential for danger that presented itself on this series of voyages and, as the originator of the mission, I felt a heavy responsibility as we assembled both our equipment and our people.

Reflecting on what lay ahead, I thought back to two previous expeditions that involved danger—our long exploration of the Amazon and our more recent work throughout the islands and the interior of Papua New Guinea. Both were larger in terms of area and logistics, but neither was tinged with more potential for sensational encounters. In Amazonia we had peered into the antiquity and exuberance of pristine nature, roaming a jungle of storied diversity that was filled with native tribes barely contacted and with unknown species of plants and animals. In Papua New Guinea we glimpsed the antiquity of humanity itself, visiting among peoples of astonishing diversity who were barely removed from the Stone Age.

Now, we would sail out to encounter an ancient creature without parallel on earth, in many ways the essence of human nightmares across the ages. Our subject now was not merely the great white shark, but the eternal relationship between man and beast, in its most elemental state and its most dramatic collision.

ABOVE:
Round-the-clock observations required that all hands carry out multiple tasks. Here, chef Bruno Gicquel, who also served as a diver and deckhand, photographs arriving great whites while suspended from Alcyone's crane.

LEFT:
Chief diver Steve Arrington rides the clear cylinder as it is lowered into position. The height of the cage precluded entry on deck, so divers were forced to slip into the plastic cage while underwater, a maneuver that exposed them briefly to possible shark attack.

RIGHT:
To test the response of white sharks to a diver seemingly unprotected in the sea, the team fashioned an experimental cage from a clear, bulletproof plastic called LEXAN. Girded by bars at top and bottom, the single sheet of plastic appeared nearly invisible underwater.

TWO HOW TO HELP A WHITE SHARK FIND YOU

*The shark passed slowly,
first the slack jaw with the
triangular splayed teeth,
then the dark eye,
impenetrable and empty as
the eye of God, next the
gill slits like knife slashes in
paper, then the pale slab of
the flank, aflow with silver
ripplings of light, and
finally the thick short
twitch of its hard tail. Its
aspect was less savage than
implacable, a silent thing of
merciless serenity.*

PETER MATTHIESSEN

Blue Meridian

It is virtually impossible to find a great white shark in the obsurity and vastness of the sea. Arrangements must be made for the shark to find *you*.

We would prefer to slip unobtrusively into the white shark's milieu and watch the creature go about its business undistracted by our presence. The purity of such observations in the wild would be priceless. But the chances of encountering a great white shark through happenstance are incalculable.

We would have to attract great whites to *Alcyone* through some kind of baiting process. This would mean that the water space into which we drew whites would be polluted by a concentration of tastes and odors unlikely in the natural world. The behavior we studied might, therefore, be both abnormal in itself and further compromised by our presence, but there was no alternative. We would have to do as others have done in order to come eye-to-eye with a great white shark.

What others have done is to create the deception that their ship is a wounded whale. The artifice is twofold: by anchoring

Two Cousteau divers seem engulfed in a cloud of blood. Despite the volume of chum initially poured in the water, days sometimes passed before great whites arrived. Eventually, the team standardized chum delivery, permitting scientists to more precisely study the shark's behavior in response to the attractants.

*Australian Rodney Fox, once a
white-shark attack victim and
now a champion of protection for
the species, prepares his special
shark chum of blood and tuna*
*bits on Alcyone's rear deck.
Before marine mammal laws
were enacted, fishermen seeking
whites often killed sea lions for
bait, or chummed with whale oil.*

a vessel one presents an image that arriving sharks might
mistake for a dead or dying whale along the surface; by pouring
blood and other animal matter into the water one simulates
bodily fluids leaking from the whale.

Before the decline of whaling, and the imposition of stringent
marine-mammal protection laws, Australians who sought great
whites used whale meat and oil to attract the sharks. There is
evidence that white sharks in some parts of the world relish
whale meat. In the north Atlantic, whites have been observed
feeding on the floating carcasses of dead whales, and bite marks
found on whales suggest they may even gouge meat from living
animals. Many years ago, when whaling vessels routinely
pulled into Durban, South Africa, anglers were able to catch

great whites commonly from piers at the entrance to the harbor. Presumably, the whites were attracted to the remains cast off the whaling vessels, perhaps following the ships into the harbor. When whaling dwindled in the sixties, and eventually ended, the catches of great whites also declined.

We heard reports that some Australians who hope to film or capture whites still retain a clandestine supply of whale products, but we were bound by conscience to avoid such bait. To concoct a recipe likely to entice great whites we sought the help of a man who has attracted, and surely observed, more great white sharks than anyone in the world. During the past three decades, Australian Rodney Fox has led some thirty-five major expeditions to film or to study great white sharks off South Australia. Although he is not a trained scientist, Rodney has been a devoted diver and a keen observer of the undersea world since childhood. But his fascination with the great white shark comes not from any abstract whim. While diving nearly thirty years ago, Rodney was attacked by a white shark in such dramatic fashion that his survival was miraculous, and his story is forever fixed in the lore of the great white shark. Some would have forsworn diving in the aftermath, but Rodney's curiosity was fueled and he has spent most of his life trying to learn more about the creature that nearly killed him.

When I met Rodney I avoided asking him to relate the details of his attack. There would be plenty of time later to hear his story. I wanted to know if he would consider joining our expedition and I described our purpose. He is a soft-spoken man with a lively intelligence, and I saw his eyes light up with excitement.

Rodney told me he had begun to feel somewhat guilty about the menacing image of the great white. He had served as a guide and consultant during the filming of live-action scenes for the movie *Jaws*. He now considers it the worst job he ever took.

"I didn't know it would be a horror film," he told me. "Now I find that many people have given up diving and swimming after seeing the film. It was a fictional story, but people believed it. And it isn't only *Jaws*. All the film companies I've been involved with for the past twenty years have portrayed the great white smashing into cages and biting baits, emphasizing their most savage look. Nobody portrays them normally—just swimming beautifully through the water. The world has seen the nasty side of the great white and not the good side."

With Rodney's help, we would try to capture an honest portrait of an animal elevated to the role of demon in the public's mind.

We began our quest mid-April 1989, loading *Alcyone* under the cool breezes of the austral autumn in Port Adelaide. After filling our freezer and our below-deck pantry with food, stowing the crew's gear, and hauling aboard the new cylindrical LEXAN cage—built in Adelaide under Rodney Fox's supervision—we headed across Gulf St. Vincent and Spencer Gulf to Port Lincoln, a small fishing village that would serve as our staging area.

Here, an already crowded deck came to resemble a miniwarehouse. In addition to a Zodiac and an aluminum dinghy, electric scooters, Comsat satellite antenna, and assorted piles of diving, scientific, and deck gear, we had to find room for the two antishark cages and half a dozen shrimp boxes. Rented from the Port Lincoln fishing fleet, these four-foot-square containers would serve as bait boxes for Rodney's special shark-attracting *bouillabaisse*.

The arrival of a melange—more than a ton in all—of various kinds of chum marked a change in our life aboard *Alcyone* that would persist throughout the expedition. We would live with a noxious stench. We would not only imitate a dead whale, we would smell like one. To bring the bait aboard, we formed a chain of crewmen from the wharf down the gangplank to the deck, and as the chum was passed along the line, I watched faces turn sour, eyes roll, heads shake in disbelief. The mixture was formidable: the recipe consisted of fish heads, minced blue fin and skipjack tuna, as well as whole fishes and tuna oil, containers of both wet and dried blood, and raw horsemeat. Dried blood, we learned from Rodney, is commonly used as fertilizer and also as a foaming agent in firefighting chemicals. The horsemeat, obtained from a pet food company, peaked our curiosity. Why horsemeat? Rodney smiled. He had no idea why, but it was markedly superior to beef in attracting sharks.

The excitement of searching for great white sharks was quickly tempered by the repugnance of the gifts we would offer them. In the days to come we would endure sickening gusts of foul odor swirling about us in the breeze and would wince as blood streaked *Alcyone*'s white decks.

Our spirits were lifted, however, when several Port Lincoln fishermen sailed by to express support for our mission, and to welcome us to the area with presents of fresh tuna, not for the sharks but for our own consumption.

Before embarking, we welcomed aboard the final essential tool, a scientific mind capable of assessing shark behavior. Months earlier I had invited an old friend, Don Nelson, to accompany us on the shark search. Nelson is a professor of biology at California State University, Long Beach, where he researches the behavior, ecology, and sensory biology of sharks and rays. Whenever time permits, Nelson and his students study their subjects in the field, and his published papers appear in the most prestigious journals and books. Nelson is famous among his peers for a series of innovative studies of gray reef sharks, *Carcharhinus amblyrhynchos*, considered the boldest, most aggressive shark around the coral atolls of Polynesia and Micronesia. He and colleague Richard H. Johnson were the first to study in detail a type of threat display common to gray reef sharks in the moments before they launch an attack. When cornered, the sharks arch their backs, raise their snouts, and lower their pectoral fins. With aides, Nelson developed a one-person, fiberglass shark observation submersible, enabling his team to witness attacks at the closest possible range—from within a tiny submarine as it became the object of a gray shark's apparent anger. Years ago Nelson had shown me film taken from within the sub, which was attacked some ten times, sustaining minor damage from the sharks' lightninglike strikes.

Nelson's curiosity about white sharks stemmed from an incident several years ago in the Florida Keys when he came upon one unexpectedly during a dive. The great white immediately fled. Nelson suspects that most white shark attacks on people are not the result of aggressive behavior such as defending territory, but rather that they are merely investigative bites by a hungry animal.

Aboard *Alcyone*, Don could team up with Rodney to provide us with experienced eyes; they would be sensitive to shark behavior patterns our crew might not notice.

On the afternoon of April 19, we set out on a southeasterly course from Port Lincoln, arriving at dusk along the two tiny plots of land known as Dangerous Reef. As one of our staff members in the United States wrote when faxing *Alcyone*, the name sounded like a setting in a Hardy Boys adventure. Yet the name had nothing to do with great white sharks. It was bestowed by early sailors who saw in these low, rocky mounds a peril for ships during rough or foggy weather.

No one is quite certain why great whites can be found here. Rodney's years of searching have identified Dangerous Reef as the most likely site in South Australia to find them. He always begins here, then moves to other islands if none appear. He describes the reef as a calling place for the whites, and suspects that whether they are traveling northward to the shallower water of the gulfs, or southward toward deeper water, they tend to congregate at Dangerous Reef.

There is a more tangible explanation, and we could hear it as we approached the islands. A colony of Australian sea lions, *Neophoca cinerea*, lives on Dangerous Reef, one of the few havens left for the animals, which have been vastly reduced in number by human hunting. There may be only about 10,000 in existence. They are a handsome species with smooth, palomino coats. The conventional wisdom assumes that white sharks seek out Dangerous Reef to prey upon these sea lions and their pups when they enter the water.

We anchored along the lee side of the islands, where the water was only about eighty feet deep. One factor in the decision was safety. Should an accident occur during our diving—such as the snapping of a cage cable—the equipment and personnel would be within easy rescue, even if they dropped to the bottom.

Immediately Rodney began creating his plume of blood and tuna oil in the water off the stern. He also tossed a few lines out with a tuna head and a balloon tied to the end of each. The balloons act principally as warning devices. When they suddenly disappear from the surface, one can surmise that a shark has taken the bait. The bait trail would be maintained through the night and until it bore results. Peering down into the stained waters, I watched the arrival of hundreds of small silver fish, cousins of the Australian salmon known locally as tommy roughs. Perhaps when a white shark came along they would disperse, but until then the ocean ceiling was raining a feast of fish fragments, sending them into a ravenous swarm.

Captain Dourassoff posted a schedule of four-hour watches for the crew, tacking up alongside it the directions for mixing the chum, or burley, as Australians call it. To their regular routine of checking the anchored ship for leaks, fires, drifting off course, approaching vessels, and weather developments, the team would soon be accustomed to the tedium of steadily pouring a malodorous mixture into the sea.

My experience has been that the ocean is ever deceptive. Whatever one expects when setting out on an expedition will prove to be a misjudgment, as if there was a mind at work in the waters maliciously disappointing or confusing those of us along the surface. Rodney had told us it could take several days to attract whites and we arrived at Dangerous Reef prepared for a long wait. We were surprised almost immediately by their appearance and then, when hopes were high, by their disappearance.

Shortly after dawn on our first morning at the reef, Rodney's normally subdued voice boomed out "Shark! Shark!" Paul Martin rang the dinner bell—our prearranged signal to alert the crew to the presence of a shark—and every bunk on the ship emptied quickly. By the time we had all reached the stern, Rodney was pointing to a dun-colored, torpedolike shape in the water. The creature was moving slowly in a great circle, gliding beneath *Alcyone* and then surveying the chum-saturated waters at the stern. Rodney estimated the length at about eleven feet, but couldn't see if the shark had the telltale male sexual organs called claspers behind the anal fin, the only obvious marks of

A reconnaissance party of Australian sea lions inspects Cousteau divers near Hopkins Island, where the team was able to dive without cages to observe them. Once nearly extinct, the species is now protected and increasing in number and range.

A young fur seal strikes an endearing pose on North Neptune Island. Entering the sea, awkward youngsters like this become a favored prey of great whites. The appearance of fur seals led early sailors to call them sea bears.

Diver Capkin Van Alphen and an Australian sea lion regard one another cautiously. For the Cousteau team, such encounters approximated what the great white shark sees in its liquid hunting grounds—an acrobatic prey that may be wily enough to escape all but surprise attacks.

Two Australian sea lions seem unbothered by the crowd of cormorants and gulls sharing Dangerous Reef. Most specialists believe that great whites congregate offshore to prey upon the island's sea lion colony.

gender. The shark had my attention, of course, but I couldn't help noting that the little tommy roughs seemed unconcerned about its presence. They continued to lurch through the chum.

Then suddenly the white swept upward easily to engulf an entire three-foot-long tuna from a bait line, and the tommy roughs briefly parted along its path. For a moment the shark thrashed its head from side to side, pulling the fish free, and then quickly dived out of sight toward the bottom.

I turned to Louis Prezelin, who was holding his light meter up to the emerging sunshine. He shook his head. The light would

not be sufficient yet for filming underwater. Antoine Rosset arrived with the surface camera, and Prezelin spent a few minutes trying to capture shots of the shark emerging from the gloom to lunge for bait. Our strategy was determined by Rodney, who suggested we allow arriving sharks to take a bait or two. In his experience, this immediate success and the lack of apparent danger encouraged sharks to hang around, sometimes all day. But to avoid wasting bait or satisfying the creatures, we would then try to pull away the bait lines just in advance of succeeding strikes, the marine equivalent of a

Like Greenly Island, most of the landfalls patrolled by great whites at the mouth of Spencer Gulf are rocky and barren, inhospitable to humans and inhabited principally by sea birds, pinnipeds, lizards, and snakes.

carrot-and-stick routine.

This time, the strategy failed. By the time we had enough sunlight to descend in the cages to film, the shark was gone. Nevertheless, we had indeed seen our first great white shark, and a momentous decision faced us. As is customary aboard Cousteau vessels, animals under study receive nicknames. What should we call our first visitor? Someone jokingly suggested that we name the creature after our founder—as the employees of a corporation might—and our first great white shark was accordingly dubbed *JYC*.

By the time it was certain that *JYC* had vanished to wherever white sharks go, we had already proceeded with our preparations to film him. With the crew suited up and the cages ready to be lowered, we decided to make two test dives. We would check out the equipment, become accustomed to it, and hope that, perhaps intrigued by the activity, *JYC* might return to observe the commotion. He did not.

We returned to the surface and went through the hour-long process of cleaning and stowing the gear. Just as we finished, the dinner bell rang out. Rodney was pointing to another great white off the stern, estimating its length at thirteen feet. We raced about again, madly reassembling ourselves as underwater shark filmers, but the creature lingered only for a few minutes. By the time we were again prepared to dive, the second shark had followed the first into the endless haze of the undersea horizon. In light of the criterion used to name the first shark, the second was christened *Jean-Michel*. It is a rather odd feeling, knowing that somewhere in the sea there is a great white shark bearing your name. But the honor was soon forgotten. We never again saw either *JYC* or *Jean-Michel*.

Yet our spirits soared. In only twelve hours of chumming we had already attracted two sharks. This was easy stuff, after all. We turned again to the drudgery of chumming and scanning the horizon, waiting for the next great white to appear at any moment. In fact, the next one would not arrive for six days.

During our second night on Dangerous Reef, the wind rose and the seas kicked up. South Australia is at the mercy of storms propelled northward from the Antarctic, and weather forecasting can be a dicey business. We had elected to leave our cages in the water, but by morning on the second day we were forced to secure them to the deck. The immense strain exerted on the cage lines by *Alcyone*'s heaving could break a cable. We continued to chum, but Rodney was not optimistic. He believes great whites dislike storm-swollen surface waters as much as humans do, and that when the water is choppy they retreat to the more tranquil waters near the bottom.

Bait meant to draw great whites to Cousteau cages often attracted other fish, such as these juvenile chinaman leatherjackets. Relatives of the triggerfish, they aggressively pestered divers, even nipping at their feet through cage floors. Curiously, with the exception of four bronze whalers (Carcharhinus brachyurus), *only great whites appeared in the chum-saturated waters at Alcyone's stern—although many shark species frequent the area.*

The next few days wore on, gray and windy and surging with heavy swells. Out of frustration, the crew turned to those maintenance tasks set aside for spare time at sea. Australian Capkin Van Alphen, our newest diver and deckhand, patrolled the ship with the sanding and painting tools of rust prevention. At six-feet-five inches tall and twenty-two years of age, he was the biggest, strongest, and youngest aboard. A diver since the age of ten, he roamed *Alcyone* with the bounding enthusiasm of a giant child playing on an immense new Christmas toy. Our only problem with Capkin was that his restless muscles and herculean frame burned fuel at a high rate. His resultant appetite was as outsized as his personality, forcing Bruno Gicquel to prepare fifteen meals for a crew of twelve.

Wandering the ship, I watched each man tending to his special responsibilities. Chief diver Steve Arrington spent hours sorting through the medical supplies aboard, noting which drugs or bandages were old or in short supply. Aboard *Calypso* there is room for a doctor, but on *Alcyone* we rely on a crewman with extensive first-aid knowledge. With fourteen years as a bomb-disposal frogman in the U. S. Navy, and years of experience supervising a recompression chamber, Arrington meets our qualifications. In his California home there is a Naval Commendation Medal bestowed for saving five lives during his service career.

To our engineers, Paul Martin and Joe Cramer, *Alcyone* is a floating machine shop, and they busied themselves tuning the generator engines and the outboard motors. Cramer, like most of us, retires to his quarters during off hours to read or write letters home, but Martin leans across the stern life raft for hours at a time with a rod and reel, helping to supplement our food supply with fresh fish. I've eaten meals caught by Paul from Gibraltar to the Amazon.

The absence of sharks has little bearing on the continual work of the captain and the navigator, Dourassoff and Stern. The log must be kept, the weather reports monitored, the duties assigned. There are slow times, however, during which they inventory the charts or supervise the restowing of the line locker, where mooring lines and fenders are kept.

Yet we were not in the South Seas for ship's maintenance. We were here to study sharks. After two more days of waiting at Dangerous Reef, we decided to try other locations, and followed Rodney's directions north to islands in the Sir Joseph Banks Group, to no avail, then south to the Neptune Islands. Anchoring off South Neptune at dinner time, we again created an "odor corridor" of chum off the stern, then gathered for one of Gicquel's four-star meals.

I sensed boredom as I looked around the table in the *carré*, so I asked Rodney to regale us with the story of his near-fatal white shark attack. For an hour we sat in rapt attention, enthralled not only by the story but by Rodney's fluid way of telling it.

In 1963, Rodney was a newly married twenty-two-year-old, making a living as an insurance salesman but consumed by his passion for diving and for spearfishing. He was the reigning male spearfishing champion in Australia, and the favorite to win the South Australian Championship, which was held December 8 at Aldinga Bay, about thirty miles south of Adelaide.

Four hours into the event, Rodney was free-diving about a thousand yards offshore. Some forty other spearfisherman were hunting, and since a great many fish had been taken there was blood in the water. No one had speared as many fish as Rodney and he appeared likely to win. Seeing a dusky morwong—a large, perchlike bottom fish—Rodney approached for the kill that would ensure victory. With his left arm raised for stability, he aimed the gun to fire.

"All of a sudden," Rodney told us, "a huge thump hit me in the chest. It knocked the gun out of my hand and the mask off my face, and I was just hurled through the water at great speed.

That was my greatest impression at first, that I was traveling faster through the water than I ever had. I quickly realized that it must have been a shark, and that the shark was holding me as a dog holds a bone, so I gouged around its head, knowing that its eyes would be the only vulnerable spot. As I tried to poke its eyes, it suddenly pulled back. I thrust my right hand at its face to ward it off, and my hand disappeared over its teeth, ripping my hand so badly that it would eventually be closed by ninety-seven stitches.

"Quickly, I pulled my hand out before it could be chewed off, and I thought: I'll grab it in a bear hug. So I put both arms around it—away from its head so that it couldn't bite me. But I was snorkeling, and I simply ran out of air. I knew that I would drown any second, so I pushed off from the shark and kicked myself upward to the surface with all my strength. I took two or three very big gulps of air, and then I looked down."

Rodney paused, looking about the faces at the table, shaking his head. "What I saw was the nightmare we all worry about, and I cannot ever forget it. There below me the water was all blood red, and a huge head with its mouth open was coming up to eat me. That was the terrifying moment of the experience.

"I kicked at the shark as hard as I could, and the shark spun around. Instead of biting me again, it swallowed a nylon buoy that I was towing behind me with one fish on it. As the shark continued its circle, it came to the end of the buoy cord, which

In 1963, in one of Australia's most famous white shark attacks, spearfishing champion Rodney Fox suffered wounds that required 462 stitches. Fox survived to become a student of white shark behavior.

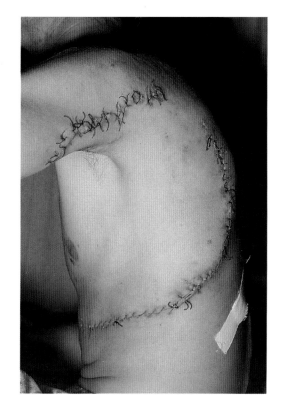

Perched as a shark lookout atop the forward Turbosail cylinder, chef Bruno Gicquel alerts the team to a great white approaching the port side.

Anne-Marie, *an eleven-foot* *female, thrusts into the air in pursuit of bait. Team members occasionally allowed whites to take a bait in order to maintain their interest without satisfying their hunger. Almost as frequently, however, the sharks struck quickly enough to take the bait before it could be hauled in.*

was attached to my belt, and suddenly I was being towed downward through the water. The shark went faster and faster, and I was swirling uncontrollably behind him. I tried to grab my quick-release belt to free myself, but the release had slipped around to my back, out of reach. Again I was about to drown, or to die from the wounds, and I had given up, when all of a sudden the buoy cord snapped. Apparently, when the shark had first bitten me, he had cut halfway through the cord. Now, under great pressure, the line broke and I was free. I managed to drift up to the surface, and when I emerged I yelled out, 'Shark! Shark!' as hard and as loud as I could."

Miraculously, a rescue boat had spotted the clouds of blood and was heading in Rodney's direction to investigate at the moment he surfaced. He was quickly pulled in, with blood pouring from his wetsuit, and rushed to shore. There, while a stranger held his intestines in place, he was transferred to a car, which was soon met by an ambulance, and he was admitted to a hospital for emergency surgery within an hour of the attack. The teeth of the white shark had left gaping holes in Rodney's torso, revealing his stomach, lungs, and ribs, many of which were cracked. The circle of punctures extended up his left arm, which was open to the bone. The wounds required 462 stitches, but Rodney survived. In fact, he and a partner won the team spearfishing championship only a year later, and soon Rodney was making his living as an abalone diver in waters known to harbor great white sharks.

"I don't feel any malice toward the white shark," Rodney said. "I'm not very happy with the one that bit me, but I don't believe they're man-eaters. I think they cause problems by biting people now and again by mistake, but it's no reason to kill them off."

"But why would you care?" I asked. "After all, a white shark nearly killed you."

"I think they're beautiful animals," he said, "and I believe we

must try to understand them better. I feel sorry for them. I don't think we should kill off a species just because we fear them."

Throughout Australia, where beaches are a way of life and sharks are a pervasive worry, Rodney's attack dominated the news and he was an instant celebrity. People stopped him on the street, eager to see his scars.

"The media still ring me up at the beginning of each summer here, and they say: 'We've heard that the gulfs are full of sharks this year. Would you like to make a comment?' And if I tell them the truth, that white sharks seem to be declining, they don't report it. If I say: 'Oh, there could be a few more this year,' then the story escalates into a major front-page warning."

So concerned are Australians with the threat of sharks roaming their beaches that the country instituted an unprecedented protection program more than fifty years ago. Prior to 1937, Australia had the highest incidence of shark attacks in the world. To calm public fears, the New South Wales government devised a system of shark netting—also called meshing—that was set up at intervals along the beaches of Sydney, Newcastle, and Wollongong, where most of the attacks

had taken place. Held to the bottom by lead weights, the nylon gill nets are about 500 feet long and 20 feet deep. They are set parallel to beaches about a thousand feet offshore, sometimes farther. Though there are many gaps between the nets, and the lowering of the nets is done periodically, the system has proved remarkably effective. In the twenty-one years prior to meshing, there were twenty-seven shark attacks along New South Wales beaches. In the fifty years since, there have been two. This record of success prompted the introduction of similar meshing programs in Durban, South Africa, in 1952 and in Queensland, Australia, in 1962. To date, no other beaches in the world are similarly protected by extensive netting.

Yet there are problems with the system. Some researchers believe that the nets succeed by depleting the shark populations in the region to near extinction. And the captured sharks, most of which are dead, are not treated as a resource but are casually dumped at sea, eliminating the possibility for scientific studies. The greatest problem may be that the nets are not discriminatory; other harmless animals are trapped and killed in them. Since 1962 in Queensland alone nets have caught 468 dugongs, 2,654 turtles, 317 dolphins, and two whales.

OPPOSITE:
Once plagued by the world's highest incidence rate of shark attacks on swimmers, Australia began fencing off many beaches in 1937 using mesh nets lowered in the shallows a few hundred yards offshore. Though the nets are not continuous, they have nearly eliminated attacks where employed. Unlike most captured sharks, which die in the nets, this great white was found alive in meshing along a Queensland beach and released.

Jean-Michel examines a shark warning sign at a beach near Sydney. Until protective mesh netting was introduced in the 1930s, Australia had the highest incidence of shark attacks in the world. Yet of nearly 500 attacks recorded during the past 200 years in all of Australia, only twenty are known to have involved great white sharks.

Relatively few great white sharks end up in the nets. Between 1949 and 1990, only about eleven have shown up in the nets each year, and nearly all were immature. In fact, catches of great whites have steadily declined since the introduction of meshing. No one can say whether this is a result of the net captures or other factors, but it is disconcerting to those who, like Rodney, believe that the whites are disappearing.

These records increase our doubts about the reputation of great whites. Throughout the world, whites are blamed for more attacks on humans than any other species. Yet often no clear identification of the attacking sharks has been made. Further, most attacks occur in tropical waters where great whites are rarely sighted. Many of these incidents may actually involve bull and tiger sharks, which are common in the tropics and are known to have attacked people and boats.

Moreover, great white attacks on humans are rarely fatal. Along the coast of California and Oregon, some 33 white shark attacks on humans have been recorded in the past 53 years. Of these, only four proved fatal, and in each case the victim was not eaten but died from loss of blood after being pulled from the water. The most likely explanation is that white sharks bite humans by mistake and withdraw, or bite simply to inflict a major wound and then back off to wait while the victim grows weak. Many researchers believe that such a strategy could enable whites to disable large prey such as sea lions without risk. A struggling pinniped could bite and harm a shark during a sustained battle, but a wounded sea lion would likely be incapacitated by the loss of blood after a period of time, making it easier to consume.

By the morning of April 26, the storm had abated and our spirits rose. There were no sharks at the bait lines, but the sea was relatively flat off South Neptune Island, and we decided to break the monotony with another test dive in the cages. Dourassoff supervised the preparation of the cages, Van Alphen the diving gear. Just when all was ready, we heard Thierry Stern shouting and pointing at one of the bait lines. It was severed and drifting on the surface with neither bait or balloon. Then came the cry we had awaited for days. "Shark!" yelled Stern, pointing to a dark shape passing beneath our aluminum dinghy. Rosset passed our new 35mm underwater camera to Prezelin, who leaped into a cage. Our plan was to send a lookout diver with the cameraman at all times. Armed with a plastic billyclub, the lookout would provide another set of eyes while the cameraman was busy filming. For this first shark dive, Arrington would act as lookout, and when he climbed in, the cage was quickly lowered.

From above, we were able to identify the shark as a young male about ten feet long. He seemed cautious, swimming in wide circles, probably perplexed by the arrival in his world of a square-shaped object emitting clouds of bubbles. Eventually, he approached the stern again and with slow but powerful tail strokes slid upward to gulp a two-foot tuna in a single bite.

Below, Prezelin and Arrington had a different impression. Though young, the white seemed enormous. Rodney had warned us that divers are always unprepared for the size of a white shark. Older sharks, especially, seem extraordinarily wide. It is believed that their growth pattern changes at some point, that they may not continue to grow longer but increase in girth, so that an older shark has a tremendous chest.

As the minutes passed and the shark maintained his distance from the cage, Prezelin gave three tugs on a rope that acted as a messenger line to the surface. The cage was lowered fifteen feet farther. Seemingly more confident, the white now came closer to investigate the strange apparatus hanging before him. He headed toward the observation gap in the cage, where Prezelin held his camera, then suddenly veered upward and tried to bite one of the two metal floats fastened to the top of the cage. The strike was neither rapid nor ferocious, and the white quickly

turned away. Yet his curiosity seemed piqued. For several minutes he swam back and forth directly over and within inches of the cage.

Now Prezelin, eager to capture a close shot of one of these sorties, poked his head, arms, and camera through the cage port. From the beginning of our expedition planning, we had wondered about the possibility of a small shark managing to slip into the cage through this space. Rodney had assured us that he had seen no white sharks that small in these waters. But now Prezelin encountered an unanticipated problem. Suddenly the shark glided downward on a direct line toward his head. Arrington grabbed the cameraman in warning, and Prezelin began to draw back into the cage. Ever the professional filmmaker, Prezelin wore his underwater light meter like a necklace around his neck, and as he lurched back to safety, the light meter caught on the metal bars of the cage. As the shark passed, Prezelin's head was left protruding into the water like bait. The shark passed without apparent interest.

On the deck above, Don Nelson tossed a special bait line into the water. He had encased within the body cavity of a tuna a transmitter that puts out 40 kilohertz pulses, producing a characteristic pinging sound. Using an underwater telemetry receiver, the pulses can be picked up as far as a mile away. Similar experiments with other species of sharks have shown that the animals are not hurt by the device and eventually regurgitate it. If Nelson could encourage the white shark to swallow the transmitter-laden tuna, we could attempt to track the shark and gather clues about its daily movements and habits.

Rodney poured a cloud of blood into the water near the special bait and, after several passes, the shark took the tuna, triggering a volley of cheers from the team on deck.

With such a cooperative subject on hand, Nelson rushed to assemble another experiment. He had recorded artificial sounds resembling the erratic and intermittent noise produced by a struggling fish or one that is enveloped in a feeding frenzy. By playing the tape through an underwater speaker, he had successfully attracted species of reef sharks, as well as a mako shark, a close relative of whites. Yet the experiment had never been attempted before with great whites.

Unfortunately, the watery environment at our stern, crowded with equipment and flushed with blood, afforded a poor test area. The shark seemed uninterested in the speaker, passing stolidly at a distance without investigating. Nelson was not surprised, since the variety of demands on the animal's sensory system—smells, tastes, new sights, new sounds—probably represented a confusing circus of stimuli. Yet an odd thing occurred. Some twenty minutes after Nelson had given up and turned his tape machine off, the shark approached the stilled speaker and nudged it. Coincidence, or a latent curiosity about sounds heard from the speaker earlier? "Who knows," said Nelson.

For nearly two hours the shark remained near our stern, giving us ample time to consider a name for him. Since it was a male, I was moved to christen him *Philippe*, after my late brother. Philippe Cousteau grew up fascinated by sharks, and deeply appreciated their grace and beauty in the sea. His love for the animals was evident in the underwater footage he captured of them, and in the eloquence of his 1970 book *The Shark*. Were he alive today Philippe would be holding the camera in the cage below us, thrilled by his proximity to the greatest of all sharks.

As the late afternoon light waned *Philippe* could be seen turning from *Alcyone*, heading away. Nelson and I carried telemetry equipment into the dinghy and gave chase. While I steered the boat, Nelson donned headphones and lowered a pole-mounted hydrophone into the water. By swinging it from side to side, he could detect the peak intensity of the transmitter's pings, and when he pointed in a direction, I set out slowly in pursuit. For several hours, as darkness settled around

Tommy roughs show little concern as Daisy *glides among them.*

Most great whites approached
Cousteau divers cautiously, often
circling in wide arcs before
attempting to take baits. Behind
the cage, the trail of blood and
chum can be seen drifting
downcurrent.

OPPOSITE:
Tiny black dots visible along this
white shark's snout are pores with
nerve connections to the brain.
Called the ampullae of Lorenzini,
they enable sharks to detect weak
electric fields, such as those
produced by electrochemical
reactions and muscle activity in
other animals. Some researchers
believe that they enable sharks
not only to locate prey hidden
beneath the sand, but to navigate
using the earth's magnetic field.

us, we were able to track *Philippe.* Eventually the pulses grew weak and we lost him. It is possible, Nelson thought, that with larger sharks such as whites we would have to attach transmitters to the exterior of the body, since the ingested transmitter seemed to relay an insufficiently strong signal.

Again buoyed by a shark encounter, we set about chumming the next morning with high expectations. The skies were clear, the sea was glassy, the chum was redolent. And nothing happened. There was no sign of a white shark all day, nor the next day. When a third sharkless day passed, we returned to Port Lincoln for provisions, spent a night docked at the fishing wharf, and returned to the Neptunes. In three days our bait attracted nothing but tommy roughs, so we sailed to Dangerous Reef, anchored, reestablished an odor corridor for three days, and still no shark arrived.

By May 14, nearly a month after the mission had begun, we called a temporary halt and returned to Port Lincoln again. We had seen only three white sharks and had filmed only one underwater. The mood aboard was glum. I decided we would take a break, look for some other filming opportunities, and return for one last chumming session.

The next day we sought out a man named Howard Tidswell, who makes his living as a professional abalone diver. Our interest was not so much in his work, or in abalones, but in a device he uses while diving. We had heard, and Tidswell confirmed, that many abalone divers in South Australia go to extreme means to protect themselves from white sharks. Accompanying Tidswell for a day, we filmed him as he descended to the sea floor in an ingenious device—a small,

one-man mobile shark cage. Fitted with buoyancy tanks and hydraulic power, the cage acts as a kind of open submarine and work station. A breathing rig to the surface gives Tidswell unrestricted bottom time, and a hot water hose attached to his wetsuit as an umbilical keeps his body warm, extending his time in the cold water. The price of the mobile cage—about $12,000—would make the device a luxury item if it were designed merely for convenience. As Tidwell attested, its purpose is to prevent his demise in the jaws of a white shark.

Such cages began to appear following a fatal white-shark attack on a South Australian abalone diver in 1974. Just off Cape Catastrophe, only fifteen miles southeast of Port Lincoln, diver Terry Manuel was struck by a white shark with such force that he was lifted from the water. The shark took off one of Manuel's legs, and the diver died before a partner could get him to shore.

Many of the sixty commercial abalone divers in the area quit the business after the attack; others began toying with ideas for a protective gadget. That soon led to the mobile cage. It is not clear how many divers use the cages today. Tidswell claims that all but a few depend on them, but others told us that most divers now descend without them, realizing the enormous odds against a white shark attack.

Rodney Fox related his own experience. While making a living as an abalone diver for eighteen years, Rodney logged more than 6,000 hours in the water. During that time he saw only two great whites, neither of which approached him. Rodney's conclusion was that whites are interested in neither abalone nor divers.

For two days, we remained in the Port Lincoln area, while the camera team made filming excursions into Port Lincoln channel. Our goal was to capture underwater footage of Australian sea lions without the hinderance of antishark cages, and we came upon a tiny island where sea lions and their pups bask. Since Fisheries personnel had never noted the presence of whites here, we made conventional dives, and, in fact, saw no sharks at all.

But the sea lions were a rare treat. Most sea lions we have encountered throughout the world are a curious, frolicking lot, but these creatures seemed extraordinarily playful. They cavorted alongside our Zodiac, then gyrated about the divers underwater. When Prezelin, Stern, and Rosset returned to the surface, they described the rendezvous as a "wild party."

On another dive, we came across a lovely creature that, despite weighing only about three ounces, may be as lethal as the great white shark. The blue-ringed octopus injects venom during its bite that has resulted in death to human victims within minutes. The creature's toxin is more potent than that of any land animal, yet the bite is almost painless and can go unnoticed until a victim succumbs, usually within an hour. Toxin researchers believe that many incidents of human death from blue-ringed octopus bites may go undetected, even by coroners, since the autopsy features are nonspecific and the bite fades after death.

As a precaution, we outfitted Thierry Stern with a thick glove impenetrable to such a bite, and he gathered a blue-ringed octopus in his hand as Prezelin filmed. Despite his careful maneuvers around the creature, Stern endured a moment of agony. Something about his face plate aroused the octopus's curiosity, and the creature jetted to the oval glass, where it settled for several minutes. Apparently disappointed, the octopus swam off without bothering the hapless Stern.

Van Alphen and American still-photographer and cameraman Chuck Davis, who would join *Alcyone* several times on our great-white-shark missions, followed Prezelin and Stern into the water. Armed with macrophotography gear, Davis was shooting closeup stills of the octopus when the creature suddenly disappeared in a green flash. Startled, Davis looked about the reef and spotted a green parrot fish yards away with blue-ringed tentacles dangling from its mouth. Davis surfaced to tell Prezelin, who was reloading the cine camera, that he needn't bother with new film. His subject had been eaten.

With only a few days left in which to film sharks, we sailed to English Island, not far from Port Lincoln, and optimistically set to chumming again. Three weeks had passed since our last encounter with a white. Our goal now was to meet up with at least one more so that we could lower our see-through plastic

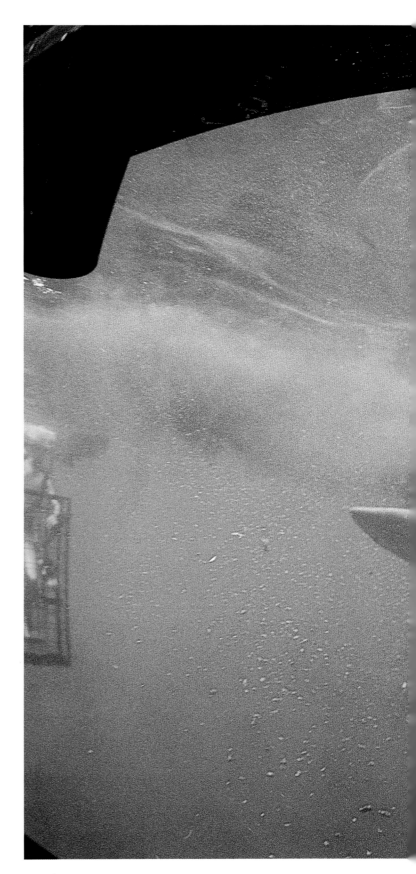

A great white photographed by cameraman and still photographer Chuck Davis shows more interest in the floats atop the diving cage than in the cloud of chum. Electrical stimulation due to galvanic currents produced by metal immersed in seawater often led the white sharks to bite Cousteau cages and other metal objects in a manner described by the team as slow, spasmodic, erratic, and even involuntary.

cage and test the shark's reactions to an apparently unprotected diver in the water.

On the afternoon of May 20, we got our wish. The arrival was a female, about eleven feet long, and she appeared eager to be a star, circling close to the stern, taking our bait and coming back for more. While the film team raced to suit up and descend, I joined Martin and Dourassoff, who were pulling in the bait lines just in advance of the shark's strikes. Excited by the opportunity after such a long wait, we were soon shouting and laughing.

Again, I found myself surprised by the shark's manner. Not ferocious, not wildly and mindlessly violent as stories have led us all to expect. Nothing like that, really. Describing my feelings to Dourassoff, I was tempted to use the word gentle, but that was not accurate either. I settled on wary, which seemed to best capture the slow, deliberate, smooth approach of the creature. There was no mistaking its potential for destruction, of course. When its huge maw opened to consume a fish, the rippling muscles in its throat bunched up like white inner tubes. The snout seemed to rise, while the jaws jutted forward to bite—a mechanism science calls jaw articulation. The mouth that maintained a strange, grinlike image when swimming suddenly turned into a protruding pincer, outfitted with upper and lower teeth that fit together in the bite like shears.

It was frightening in the moment of the bite, but before and after, this feared creature seemed no more terrible than any other. I recalled a line written by film writer Bud Weiser years before in describing another animal. "It is just another

creature," Weiser wrote, "neither good nor evil, just trying to survive."

When the steel cages were in the water, the plastic cage was lowered. We had constructed the cylinder for maximum strength: it was made from a single sheet of ³⁄₁₆-inch LEXAN plastic, curled into a four-foot-diameter tube and bolted together, with LEXAN tubes supporting both ends. Two metal pontoons in a metal frame at the top made the cylinder buoyant. In the event the cylinder should be severed from its line, the diver within could blow air into the pontoons using his Scuba, so that it would rise. We had considered several designs, arriving at what seemed the most practical and durable. Yet we had no idea what to expect. The plastic could stop a .38-calibre bullet, but could it stop a two-ton great white shark?

Among those who helped in the design was chief diver Arrington. When the cylinder arrived aboard *Alcyone* at Port Adelaide, I had asked him if he felt the novel cage was safe enough. He believed it was, unless a shark managed to drive it against the hull of the ship and crush it.

"But yes," he said. "I believe it's safe enough."

"Good," I said, "because you're the one going in it."

Now, as he prepared to enter the cylinder, I caught

Observed by a Cousteau team member, abalone diver Howard Tidswell scours the seafloor from the safety of his specially designed, mobile shark cage. Fear of great whites following a 1974 attack on a South Australian abalone diver prompted development of these protective devices. The side of the cage, opened here, can be closed when a shark is sighted.

OPPOSITE:
Rodney Fox, left, and Dr. Don Nelson test acoustic equipment prior to the Cousteau team's attempts to attract white sharks using tape recordings of wounded prey rather than blood. The trials met with limited success due to the scarcity of sharks during the first Cousteau mission at Dangerous Reef.

The Cousteau team found that individual great whites usually gave wide berth to other members of their species. Though occasionally as many as seven or eight individuals were circling Alcyone's stern, photographers were unable to capture more than two or three in their lenses at one time.

OPPOSITE:
Great white sharks are not the only dangers lurking in the waters off South Australia. The Cousteau team often encountered blue-ringed octopuses, shy creatures the size of tennis balls. A toxin they inject when biting is more potent than that of any poisonous land animal.

Arrington's eye. He smiled, shaking his head as if to say, "What a way to make a living."

Bruno Gicquel had climbed to the top of a Turbosail, from which vantage point he could keep track of the shark and give Arrington a signal to enter the water. When the shark turned away from the ship, Gicquel shouted and Arrington leaped into the water. We watched him swim quickly to the top of the plastic cage, open its double hatch doors, and squeeze in.

The shark paid little notice to Arrington in the cage at first. On her next approach, she headed for one of the metal cages and made what seemed another test bite. Then, abruptly, she veered toward the bottom of the plastic cylinder and struck a glancing blow off the bottom tube supports.

Within the cylinder, Arrington found himself engaged in a different kind of experiment—a psychological one.

"Underwater, "he would tell us later, "the single sheet of plastic between you and the shark disappears to your eye. It's like looking through a face plate. Your rational mind is aware that there is a protective wall, but you don't sense it visually, and your subconscious mind is not at all convinced. When the shark first nudged the bottom, I could see the plastic tubes bend somewhat and her snout enter the cage. Instinctively, I jerked my feet up. She was unable to break through and gobble me up but every motor response in my body seemed to believe otherwise."

On the stern above, we continued to work the bait lines, tossing and retrieving them to keep the white intrigued. While we were concerned about the safety of the men below, an incident occurred on the rear deck that briefly called into question our casual assumption that the only danger was below.

Captain Dourassoff jerked a bait line back to the starboard swimstep, which he shared with Martin, who was manning the crane. Neither was aware that the shark was chasing the bait fish at the moment, and when the fish landed on the deck, a huge shark head rocketed from the water in pursuit, mouth agape. The shark's teeth crunched into the swimstep only inches from Martin's feet, leaving quarter-inch scrapes in the metal deck as the creature slid backward into the water.

Paul Martin is a veteran seaman, calm of temperment. He rarely moves with the speed of a leaping gazelle. This time he did.

The shark remained along *Alcyone*'s flanks for three hours, during which the divers stayed below, chilled to the bone in the cold southern waters. Through the entire time, the shark displayed little interest in Arrington and his invisible cage. Eventually, Arrington tried to attract her attention by waving his arms and pounding on the cylinder walls. She remained far more interested in the dangling bait fish and the metal floats on the conventional cages.

When at last she swam off, and the cages were hauled aboard, the mood was celebratory. Prezelin was uncharacteristically effusive in describing the footage he had captured. Davis was thrilled by his opportunities to take dramatic still photos. And Arrington, while slightly disappointed

Standing precariously on the slope of Alcyone's *portside Zodiac ramp, Capkin Van Alphen keeps the interest of a great white by hauling in a bait of horse meat at the last moment.*

ABOVE RIGHT:
While comrades keep watch from a steel cage, chief diver Arrington descends into the clear plastic cylinder.

that the shark found him less interesting than fish heads, was noticeably happy to be all in one piece.

Over a dinner that evolved rapidly into a festive party, we toasted our final shark, naming her after the person who for so long kept Cousteau crews dedicated and involved, my late mother, Simone.

While in many ways the expedition had been frustrating, it had fueled our curiosity and concern for great white sharks. We had seen only four individuals in more than a month. Did this imply they are a disappearing population? We decided over champagne that we must come back to these waters equipped for an unprecedented examination of the white shark's behavior, its numbers, and its plight. We would continue to film, but we would greatly expand our research effort to acquire scientifically reliable data on these creatures.

That night, sitting alone at the chart table on the bridge as we raced toward Port Lincoln to elude an arriving storm, I reflected

on our first encounters with the most feared animal on earth. I recalled Rodney's remark, that he "felt sorry for them." Such a sentiment seemed odd as we were embarking on the mission, before we had seen the white shark for ourselves, before we had watched the creature's tentative behavior in approaching *Alcyone*, before we had marvelled at its living elegance as it swam only inches from our cameras. Now, we felt somehow involved with it. It was no longer the abstract monster of legend, but a hungry animal somewhat confused and ambivalent in our presence, searching its realm for the means to survive. The possibility that it might be vanishing from the sea worried us enormously. We had come to see *Carcharodon carcharias* as just another animal, as worthy as any of our understanding, respect, and protection. We were not surprised so much by its size or its might as by its seeming caution in the midst of human beings, and by the unanticipated empathy aroused in us.

For obvious reasons, Cousteau divers had to keep a 360° watch when great whites were present. Here, while Michel Deloire prepares to film in one direction from the LEXAN cylinder, a white appears silently from behind and below, seemingly ready to taste Deloire's fin. Fortunately, the cinematographer saw the shark in time to avert danger.

T H R E E

ENCOUNTERS WITH ROSY, ISABELLE, AND PEACHES

*Queequeg no care wat god
made him shark . . . medder
Fejee god or Nantucket
god, but de god wat make
shark must be one dam
Ingin.*

HERMAN MELVILLE
Moby Dick

On January 28, 1990, standing on *Alcyone*'s swimstep, Rocky Strong implanted a fisheries tag below the dorsal fin of a fifteen-foot-long female white shark off Dangerous Reef. The marker bore the identification number 68151 and the address of the South Australian Fisheries Department. A color-coded, spaghettilike plastic tube streamed from the tag, a modification we had devised to facilitate identification of individual sharks from the surface. Because the tag attached to number 68151 was orange and yellow, we christened her *Peaches*. She would become the first of forty white sharks eventually tagged by Cousteau teams, and because of her distinctive new emblem, the first among several we could easily recognize as regular visitors to *Alcyone*. We could not bring ourselves to refer to a fifteen-foot shark as a pet, and one of the crew claimed she had a hungry disposition, but *Peaches* became a familiar and welcome presence as we set out on the second of our South Australian-white shark expeditions.

Whether one is concerned about the potential danger to humans posed by white sharks or merely curious about the behavior of the sea's largest predatory fish, the gathering of scientific data about the animal begins with its whereabouts—by day, by night, by season, and across the course of its lifetime. The traditional means for accumulating such information is to tag wild animals and attempt to follow them through time and space. There are, to be sure, logistical difficulties in tracking animals that roam the land surface—such as elk or polar

A Cousteau diver enjoys an unobstructed view of a great white passing overhead.

Experience convinced the team that they could often safely open cage hatches to film or tag sharks.

bears—but following creatures that wander the blue obscurity of the undersea world is an extraordinary challenge. In the case of the white shark, we could observe certain individuals during the limited time available to us at sea, but after that we would have to rely on luck. Some might reappear during a future research expedition, or in the presence of a knowledgeable observer such as Rodney Fox, but it would be more likely that future information would come when a tagged white was caught by a sport or commercial fisherman.

There have been a few previous attempts to tag white sharks, but the difficulties and expense of encountering them and the rarity of recapturing tagged whites, have left us with little reliable information. One tagged South African great white travelled 481 miles in 27 days before it was recaptured. A white shark tagged off Long Island, New York, in 1984 turned up two-and-a-half years later off Murrells Inlet, South Carolina, a

distance of about 650 miles. A fifteen-foot male white tagged with a sonic transmitter was followed for eighty-three hours off Long Island in 1979. The shark was one of about five whites that was observed feeding, usually one at a time, from a dead

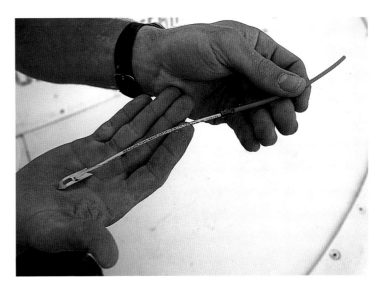

fin whale floating along the surface. For a day and a half the white remained within two miles of the whale, moving in to tear away chunks of blubber during the morning and evening. When it left the whale, the shark cruised along a meandering, generally southwesterly course, remaining for the most part at a depth of about 150 feet and covering 118 miles during two days—an average speed slightly more than two miles per hour.

Such records suggest that some whites may roam great distances, but the evidence is too sparse to be conclusive. It is entirely possible that white shark movements may vary geographically. Rodney Fox tells the story of a shark whose mangled dorsal fin made him easily recognizable. He was nicknamed *Old Bent Fin*. Rodney saw the shark on each visit to Dangerous Reef during the course of three years, and the shark appeared in several films shot from Rodney's boat. Returning to Port Lincoln one day, he spotted *Old Bent Fin* hanging from a crane on the jetty. A fisherman stood proudly alongside his catch, while a friend took the last photo ever made of *Old Bent Fin*.

Such stories lead us to suspect that many of South Australia's white sharks are local residents. It is an important question to answer, since a local population which is not replenished by arrivals from elsewhere would be more vulnerable to over-exploitation.

The tagging of *Peaches* on the first day of our second expedition seemed to fill the entire crew with enthusiasm. Cousteau Society marine biologist Rocky Strong and Barry Bruce of the South Australian Department of Fisheries had both

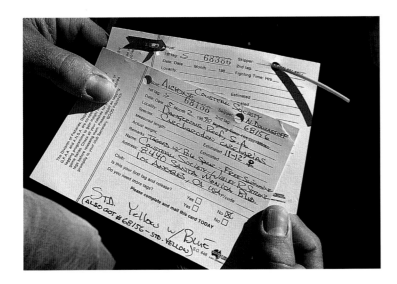

Fisheries forms completed for each tagged shark will enable researchers to gather vital information about the species' travels if tag-bearing sharks are eventually captured by fishermen. On February 5, 1990, this tag was affixed to a white shark christened Katie.

LEFT:
Tethered by a safety line, Marc Blessington implants a fisheries tag in a small great white as it rushes the stern to take a bait. The team observed great white sharks ranging from seven to eighteen feet.

ABOVE RIGHT:
The Cousteau white shark tagging program incorporated standard fisheries dart tags. To facilitate recognition of individuals, the team added color-coded lengths of polyvinyl "spaghetti" tubing to the tags. The steel barbs are designed to minimize irritation, while remaining attached to tough shark skin for long periods of time.

come aboard to direct our research program, and they trained everyone from engineer to chef in the operation of their scientific instruments. We would no longer merely toss bait and blood into the water at will. We would standardize for purposes of future scientific analysis our chum recipe, using consistent amounts of each ingredient and delivering them overboard on a regular schedule. We would also keep a close record of the conditions about us, which might affect dispersal of the chum or the behavior of the white sharks or both. Accordingly, we routinely consulted a flow meter to log the speed and direction of the currents, a thermometer to record sea-surface temperature, and *Alcyone*'s control-panel gauges to note the speed and direction of the wind.

With cinematographer Louis Prezelin dispatched to another expedition, we also welcomed aboard an old friend from Paris to conduct our filming. Michel Deloire, who began shooting Cousteau underwater footage more than 25 years ago, would take over as chief cameraman. Over the years, Michel has shot some of the most beautiful film ever taken undersea. The expedition represented a kind of poignant reunion with sharks for Michel. In 1968, with my brother Philippe, he shot most of the footage for our first television special on sharks.

Michel arrived on *Alcyone* with a shark story to tell, and the team gathered in the *carré* for the event, glasses of *pastis* all around. In dramatic fashion he described a recent dive at Catalina Island, off Southern California. He had descended with Cousteau divers Don Santee and Clay Wilcox to film sea lions amid the kelp. The team spotted several small blue sharks, and Deloire directed Santee and Wilcox to act as lookouts behind him while his camera was trained on the sea lions. About ten minutes later, Michel felt a pinch on his derriere. Sure that his two comrades were engaged in a prank, he swung around angrily. As he turned, a four-foot-long blue shark withdrew and swam away.

"The shark's teeth almost ripped through the half-inch neoprene of my suit," laughed Michel. "Had I not lost my temper and whipped around, that shark would have been a genuine pain in the butt."

Twelve hours later I was watching Michel film, not a small blue shark capable of inflicting minor wounds, but an adult great white with the capacity for mayhem. Eager for our offerings of horsemeat and blood, *Peaches* remained near us all day, giving us the opportunity to make two long dives. While Deloire filmed from one of our stainless-steel cages, and new arrival Marc Blessington was initiated into the role of lookout, Van Alphen attempted to plant a tag in *Peaches*. Opening the top hatch and rising nearly out of the cage, he tried to draw the

To remain upright for hours in the cages, Cousteau divers added a second weight belt. Cold water and the constant jostling of cages in sea swells took a toll on the divers, leading both to exhaustion and occasional seasickness. The team had to abandon diving during rough weather, for fear the pressure changes caused by sudden movements up and down could induce life-threatening embolisms.

shark near with horsemeat. As the shark passed, he released the tight rubber sling that propelled the short pole-spear bearing the tag. But each time Capkin fired the spear, it would glance off the shark's tough hide. Finally, midway through the afternoon dive, Deloire called off the tagging attempts.

With sunlight remaining, and Deloire adamant about capturing good footage of this cooperative shark, the cages remained for another hour in cold, choppy seas. To amuse himself, Capkin stuck pieces of horsemeat on the end of his plastic billyclub, offering them to *Peaches* each time she glided by. The scene had a surreal aspect to it: a boyish diver gleefully feeding a two-ton white shark from the end of a short plastic tube, as if it was a Sunday at the zoo and the creature taking the food through the cage bars was a harmless pet.

Suspended in the plastic cylinder, Steve Arrington spent the day peering into the throat of the great white and banging about in our expedition's equivalent of an amusement-park ride. Though *Peaches* displayed little interest in Arrington or his see-through cage, she returned time and again to a five-pound chunk of horsemeat hanging only two feet away. Each time, as her enormous jaws opened to engulf the meat, Arrington could see down her throat. He could even glimpse light flaring through her gill slits. Then, when a crewman topside jerked the bait line upward, forcing *Peaches* to accelerate in pursuit, the violent swinging of the shark's tail churned the water about Arrington, buffeting the cylinder and tossing the diver about like an ice cube in a martini shaker.

By late afternoon, when Deloire signalled the end of the second dive, we had still failed to affix a tag to *Peaches*. The rough seas had taken a toll on the divers. The rising and falling

action of *Alcyone* on surface swells caused the cages suspended below to lurch constantly, and the divers had spent the day battling seasickness. They emerged looking wan and chilled to the bone. Unable to warm themselves by swimming, the team suffered more than usual in the cold seas.

This unconventional diving was also exhausting. To stand upright in the cages, we had to burden the divers with an extra weight belt, adding some fifteen to twenty pounds of lead. Also, whenever a shark was present, they could not quickly grab the side of the cage to maintain their balance as the cage whipped about. To do so might risk losing part of a hand to an unseen white shark. Likewise, they had to be very careful in leaning against the side of the cage, for fear of losing something even more valuable. Unfamiliar with this routine, Blessington had used the cage wall as a support during the first dive, while he scribbled on a plastic noteboard. Without his knowledge, *Peaches* approached, seemingly ready to take a test bite of the silver body partly exposed through the cage camera port. Pausing in his notetaking, Marc happened to turn his head in thought and found himself eye to eye with a great white shark. He leaped to the center of the cage.

While great whites, like many shark species, cannot stop swimming for long periods without suffocating, the Cousteau team saw several individuals hover briefly and even back up along the bottom, apparently while searching for a meal. They extract needed oxygen, of course, through their gills. Gill slits, which can be seen in front of the pectoral fin on this great white, mark an essential difference between sharks and bony fishes: fish have one gill slit on each side, sharks betweeen five and seven.

While the divers sought hot showers, the rest of us remained on the stern. *Peaches* continued to chase our bait lines, so Strong quickly assembled a longer version of our tagging spear. Just before dark he managed to implant a spaghetti tag firmly. An identification sheet was filled out recording the time and place of the tagging and detailing any recognizable marks on the shark (*Peaches* bore only a strangely discolored, textured patch on the starboard side of her dorsal fin and a tattered edge at the rear of the dorsal). When our expeditions were completed, copies of each identification sheet would go to the Fisheries Department and would also be passed out among local fishermen, in hopes that future sightings would accumulate enough information about individual sharks to make conclusions about their movements along the southern Australia coast.

Once again, the optimism sparked by a quick shark arrival was dampened by bad weather. For more than a week, low pressure fronts followed one another across Spencer Gulf. Winds blowing twenty to thirty knots stirred up the sea, making underwater filming impossible and probably sending the sharks to the tranquil depths far beyond our blood trail.

In this dramatic photo taken by Rocky Strong in the Bahamas, a great hammerhead shark devours a southern stingray. As Strong watched, the shark used its broad head to batter and immobilize the ray, then leisurely consumed it. Curiously, the ray never wielded its stinging tail in defense. It merely attempted, unsuccessfully, to flee the attacker. Strong later drew the sequence shown at right.

The free time awaiting good weather proved valuable to us, however, since it gave the team a chance to question both of our scientists about white sharks. Rocky Strong, who discourages the use of his given name—Wesley—has worked closely with us in The Cousteau Society for several years. A North Carolina native, the young marine biologist is rapidly joining the ranks of the world's foremost experts on sharks. He has conducted extensive research on horned sharks (*Heterodontus francisci*), on the unusual ambush predation carried out by angel sharks (*Squatina californica*), and on the homing behavior of sharks in the Caribbean. Countless hours observing sharks underwater have produced some dramatic experiences, including an unprecedented moment in the Caribbean when Rocky witnessed the attack and consumption of a southern stingray (*Dasyatis americana*) by a great hammerhead shark (*Sphyrna mokarran*). The hammerhead

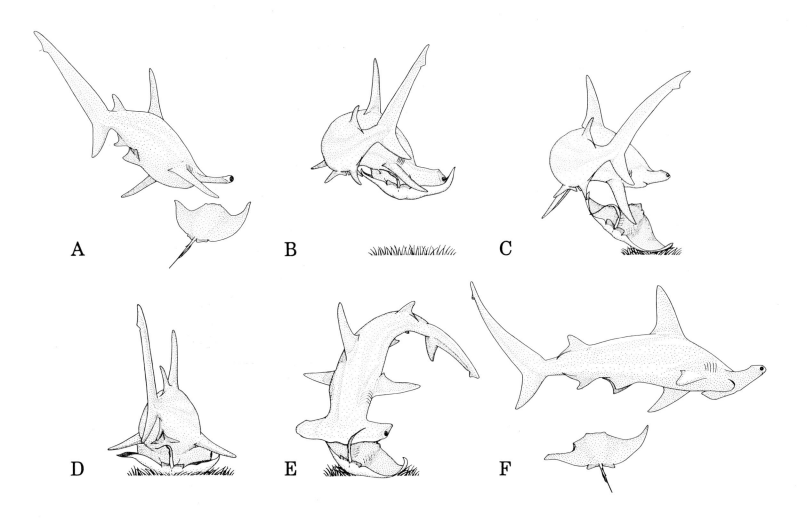

A B C

D E F

actually employed its head like a hammer to pound the victim into the bottom. The stunned ray was then leisurely consumed by the hammerhead as Rocky became the first person to witness and photograph this remarkable behavior. When the hammerhead finished its meal, Rocky watched blacktip (*Carcharhinus limbatus*) and sharpnose sharks (*Rhizoprionodon terraenovae*) scavenge on bits of the ray's carcass.

While Rocky brought a broad knowledge of sharks to our expedition, Barry Bruce served as our local specialist on great whites. While working as a senior researcher with the South Australian Department of Fisheries, Barry grew concerned about the state of the white shark population. Experienced fishermen and sailors approached him with claims that the sharks were declining in number. Though his department duties left him little spare time, Barry began gathering research on whites in 1987 and eventually proposed a department study of the creatures that were so renowned locally and yet so little understood. The program was approved and Barry was put in charge.

During the long, storm-tossed hours on *Alcyone*, Barry briefed the crew on his findings to date. Like most neophytes, we began by asking him what white sharks eat. We had read the sensational popular accounts of items found in the stomachs

of various species of sharks over the years. They range from the macabre (shoes with feet still in them), to the inexplicable (two dozen quart bottles of Vichy water bound together with a wire hoop, and a whole reindeer), to the bizarre: an 1833 account tells of a shark whose undigested remains included the headless body of a man encased in armor. The list is endless, including such oddities as license plates, a goat, a raincoat, a spaniel, a yellow-billed cuckoo, and a cow's head. The general conclusion has been that some sharks will eat anything.

Or anybody. I recalled reading in my youth the French naturalist Guillaume Rondelet, who, in 1554, had carefully considered the anatomical aspects of the biblical story of Jonah and the whale. He believed that the windpipe and lungs of a whale were so placed that swallowing a man whole would be unlikely. His candidate for the creature that gulped down Jonah was one in which, he asserted, one sometimes found whole men—the great white shark.

Barry's experience with great whites was less spectacular. During the past four years, he had examined the stomach contents of ten white sharks, all female, taken by commercial or sport fishermen along the South Australia coast. Fishermen had reported to him the contents of seven other great whites taken in the area. Of the seventeen sharks, nine had prey in their

Like a squadron of strange aircraft, scalloped hammerhead sharks pass above Cousteau divers near Cocos Island in the eastern Pacific. Like great whites, hammerheads have a reputation as man-eaters but few attacks can be directly attributed to the species.

stomachs, and eight had empty stomachs (possibly the result of regurgitation during capture in some cases).

What Barry found seemed to support the theory that the feeding preference of white sharks changes with age and size. The most common item in the larger of the analyzed sharks—from six to fourteen feet long—was dolphin remains, followed by squid, bony fish, smaller sharks, crustacea, pinnipeds, and sea birds. This did not bear out the general assumption that white sharks in the region prefer pinnipeds, such as the sea lions at Dangerous Reef, but the sample was small and the sharks had been captured in waters frequented more by dolphins than by sea lions. Smaller whites, in contrast, seemed to prefer fish, followed by some crustaceans and smaller sharks.

The difference in food preference is explained by researchers as follows: smaller great whites are more agile and their teeth are narrower, giving them the ability to pursue and grasp small, bony fishes. Larger whites, more ungainly but equipped with broader, better cutting teeth seem more adept at surprising larger mammalian prey and biting into their muscular bodies. Researchers in California have watched large great whites attack sea lions, seals, and elephant seals along the surface near the Farallon Islands, and have made interesting conclusions about the sharks' strategy. It appeared to the scientists that the sharks swam to the bottom, seemingly to conceal themselves, then attacked in a near vertical rush to surprise the prey. The pinnipeds were bitten from below and behind. Then the white sharks would move off, either to allow the victims to bleed to death or lapse into shock, returning minutes later to consume the helpless quarry.

As Barry and Rocky explained, white sharks seem to possess some remarkable biological machinery when it comes to utilization of the energy they derive from their meals. As camels in the desert have evolved ways to conserve water, white sharks may endure long periods without food. There is evidence that whites have an unusually low metabolic rate, and that their hydrodynamic form and tail-propelled method of swimming demand a relatively small expenditure of energy. Some specialists estimate that great whites may be able to survive for a month or two without eating. There are even those who believe they can last three months or longer.

When the whites do capture a meal, such as a pinniped or dolphin, they possess another biological strategy enabling them quickly to digest the food. Unlike most fish, great whites, along with their relatives the mako (*Isurus paucus*) and the porbeagle shark (*Lamna nasus*), maintain a body temperature higher than the surrounding water. This has been measured to at least nine degrees Fahrenheit in the case of great whites. The complicated anatomical machinery that makes this possible involves what

scientists call a *rete mirable*, a miraculous net, of tiny arteries and veins that return the heat generated by the shark's movements to the swimming muscles and the stomach. This principle of conserving warmth is remarkably similar to the device we call a counter-current heat exchanger. In most fish, such heat is lost through the gills.

The results of such a warm-blooded condition could be extraordinary. A warmer stomach may speed up the digestion, absorption, and assimilation of newly swallowed prey. Thus, a white shark that may go weeks or months without food can make best use of its short-lived feeding opportunities by quickly deriving energy from the sporadic meals. Treelike rings of growth in shark vertebrae often reveal spurts of growth attributable to such feeding behavior. What is not used for energy or growth can be stored away as carbohydrates in the shark's liver oil for future needs. Moreover, sporting ever-warm, ever-ready musculature, the whites may be better prepared than other fish to attack when an opportunity presents itself. John McCosker, director of San Francisco's Steinhart Aquarium and a long-time white shark researcher, compares this warmth factor in great whites to the need for a human athlete to warm up before performing. The white shark, in contrast to most fish, patrols the sea always warmed up, always ready to strike.

By February 5, the storms had abated at Dangerous Reef, and a twelve-foot female arrived at our stern promptly at 9:00 A.M. She was dubbed *Katie*, and she quickly proved to be hungry. After consuming a bait fish, she surprised us by lunging part way up the swimstep to bite a small wire cage in which we kept a store of fish heads. Crushing the cage in her jaws, she turned to leave but was restrained by a rope tethering the cage to the deck. A few seconds of wild thrashing ripped the cage free, and she descended with the dubious prize. On a later dive, we saw a mangled ball of wire on the bottom and were relieved to know that *Katie* had not swallowed the cage. As Rocky pointed out, whites are not known for swallowing the kind of inanimate objects often found in the stomachs of other species, such as the tiger shark.

Soon *Katie* was joined in the waters astern by a smaller white, *Daisy*, whom we estimated to be about nine-and-a-half feet long. Deloire and his film team quickly descended in the cages, and although the visibility was limited to about thirty feet, the two arrivals remained close enough to warrant filming. Both seemed aggressive, or hungry; it was impossible to know which. They repeatedly bit the metal floats atop the cages, and their dogged pursuit of the bait lines enabled us to tag both from the deck. They also provided the team with a good laugh. Midway through the dive, Deloire and Van Alphen found the

backup camera bouncing loosely in the cage. They set about securing it to the side with a bungee cord. In their concentration on the task at hand, they forgot to look about for the sharks. In the second cage, Davis and Blessington watched as the larger shark, *Katie*, approached the camera cage and hovered vertically with pectoral fins outstretched, only inches from the preoccupied Deloire and Van Alphen. As the shark nibbled her way along the cage toward their comrades, Davis and Blessington pulled out their mouthpieces and shouted, to no avail. Luckily, Deloire and Van Alphen caught sight of *Katie* in time to jump back from the side of the cage. Davis and Blessington, meanwhile, were consumed in laughter. Such is the strange humor of professional divers.

By evening the two sharks were gone, but they had introduced a new mystery in their appearance. Both were females, as was *Peaches* before them. Yet we had been assured that most of the white sharks we would encounter at Dangerous Reef would be males. Based on his thirty years of visiting the same waters, Rodney Fox had encountered five males for every female sighted here. Perhaps the presence of three females was a freakish occurence, or perhaps there was another explanation. Catch records suggest that white shark males and females may live their lives mostly segregated from one another. Was it possible that the ratio of the sexes had changed for some reason here at Dangerous Reef? All in all, it was an intriguing new question to attempt to answer in the coming months.

The next day passed without any shark visits. Monitoring the ship's radio, Captain Dourassoff learned that six great whites had recently been sighted at islands to the southwest, so we spent the next two days island hopping. By February 8, we had reached the Neptune Islands, where we established an odor corridor of chum and waited. The next morning a twelve-foot male arrived and was named *Wes*, after Rocky's father. We duly noted the gender, and the location—an island farther from the mainland, characterized by colder water than Dangerous Reef—and wondered if water temperature might have anything to do with the presence of males or females.

A great white nicknamed Wes *inspects a Cousteau cage and divers. Many filmmakers have portrayed such exploratory behavior as menacing, but the Cousteau team believed that the sharks were merely trying to identify unfamiliar objects. Great whites may determine if something is edible by bumping into or biting it.*

OVERLEAF:
The large volume of chum needed to lure great whites to the study area created a somewhat artificial situation, making it difficult to decipher their normal behavior. However, in a condition both similar and natural, great whites have been observed feeding around drifting whale carcasses.

Most of the great whites observed by the team bore scars and wounds, especially around the snout and head. Some of these marks may have resulted from struggles with prey or mating partners, but many appeared to be the result of the sharks' habit of investigating objects using their snouts and mouths. Still others, like this one, appeared to be natural markings.

Wes proved to be more interested in things metal than things edible. Within moments of arriving he headed for the aluminum dinghy tethered to *Alcyone*'s stern and spent fifteen minutes pushing the empty boat about with his snout. While the scene amused those of us watching from the aft deck, it was in keeping with other behavior we had witnessed and led us to question Barry and Rocky about the strange attraction of white sharks to metal. From the first expedition we had noted the way newly arriving sharks, with few exceptions, took test bites on the metal frames and floats of our cages. Filmmakers often mislead their audiences by depicting this behavior as proof of either the shark's mindless violence or its hunger-driven penchant for trying to eat anything it comes upon.

But the fact is, sharks are merely drawn to the galvanic electric currents produced by electrolysis when metal objects are submerged in seawater. Their response often appears involuntary and jerky, as if the animal were responding to a mild electric shock. The electrosensory system they use to detect prey, which is visible in the ampullae of Lorenzini— surface pores leading by canals to nerves connected to the brain—cannot distinguish between natural signals and those given off by man-made objects. At first glance, the ampullae look like beard stubble applied by a cartoonist to the snout and lower jaw, but closer inspection reveals a beautifully ordered pattern of these tiny pores.

Sharks are the most electrosensitive animals known to science. Throughout their history the ability to sense weak electric fields has led sharks to potential prey, in which electrochemical reactions and muscle activity produce such signals. With the development of metal vessels and equipment, sharks were confronted with countless opportunities for confusion. During the course of our expeditions, we saw great whites attempt to bite a zinc plate on *Alcyone*'s rudder, an outboard motor propeller, virtually every metal part of our cages, even the swimstep on several occasions.

Poring over the literature on the subject, I became fascinated with a theory proposed by several researchers that attributes to sharks a highly sophisticated and integrated system of sensing prey. The notion is that they may rely on each of their six senses in a sequential way, depending on the distance from the object of interest. Perhaps a shark first hears something, such as a struggling fish, and turns in its direction. Soon it may smell the prey, giving it another fix on the object. Following the odor corridor, it may then catch sight of the prey. Based on tissue-sectioning studies of their eyes, it is believed that great white sharks have very good distance vision, but poor closeup vision. As it approaches to within several feet of a now-visible prey, the sense of distant touch—the lateral line—may provide more refined information on the location of the quarry. At the last moment, when its vision may be imprecise and the eyes are often rolled back (or closed in species that possess eyelids), the shark may rely mostly on electroreception to guide it in the attack. When it has struck, the taste and feel of the object may help the shark comprehend what it is in the act of consuming.

Such a scenario would neatly explain why our sharks often swerved from a tuna bait at the last second to bite a cage buoy. In the excitement of pursuit, and with their vision perhaps blurred at close range, they followed electrical stimuli away from the dead fish to the galvanic current emanating from our metal cage float. Under natural circumstances, the system works marvelously, but when the shark blunders into man-made conditions, the creature cannot overcome its ancient ways and appears pathetically deceived.

Aware of the effect of metal cages on white sharks, our team had tried to minimize the phenomenon when constructing *Alcyone*'s new cages. We used stainless steel, which does not create galvanic currents on the same order of magnitude as common galvanized steel cages. Although we would sacrifice some drama in our filming, we hoped our cages would prove less harmful to the sharks. In fact, though none of our sharks grew very violent in attacking our cages, they still nibbled at the metal and took frequent test bites. As Rocky remarked after one dive, sharks simply don't have hands with which to grab and to inspect an unfamiliar object. What can they do but try to taste it or feel it at close range?

Whatever *Wes* learned about us and our gear must have been discouraging. After only an hour of chomping persistently at our dinghy and rudder, he disappeared.

After another eighteen hours of chumming at North Neptune Island with no results, we returned to Port Adelaide for provisions. There, we were surprised to find recent articles in the Port Lincoln *Times* reporting on a growing local controversy over great whites—called White Pointers by Australians because of their prominent snouts. Conservation groups had appealed to the South Australian government for a moratorium on the gamefishing of whites. A letter to the editor estimated the total population at 30 to 50—probably a low figure according to Barry, who said that most observers believe the local population probably numbers anywhere from 100 to 300. Of course, no one knows.

The issue had been inflamed recently by the capture of a female white by Australian golf star Greg Norman. Nicknamed The White Shark for his snowy mane, Norman had cooperated when producers of a sports television series proposed that he hunt with rod and reel for one of his namesakes. In answer to

calls for the end of such sportfishing of whites, the state Minister of Fisheries had decided against a moratorium because there was no evidence that the sharks were in danger of extinction. "And no evidence to say they aren't," said a Ministry spokesman, adding, "It is better to leave them as they are." A curious conclusion, I thought, realizing that our mission to help estimate the number of whites and their movements seemed more urgent than ever.

A week of chumming and waiting passed before we saw another great white. During a brief stop at Sibsey Island, where we had encountered *Simone* at the end of our first expedition, we were surveyed briefly and warily by a seven-foot female. She was the smallest white we had observed so far, and it was intriguing to find such a small shark among islands with many pinniped colonies. We would have expected the youngster to be patrolling shallower waters further north in the gulf, feeding upon bottom dwelling fish and other small sharks. Was she here to hunt pinnipeds? And if so, was she simply a precocious early starter in the hunt for bigger meals?

While she did not remain with us long enough to be tagged, she was immortalized by the crew with a distinctive name. Her evening arrival had interrupted a viewing of one of the team's favorite video cassettes—*A Fish Called Wanda*. Thus it is that a young female white today roaming somewhere in the trackless sea is in truth a fish called *Wanda*.

On the evening of February 16, we returned to Dangerous Reef. At lunchtime the next day, three sharks arrived within moments of each other and the ship came to life. There were self-congratulatory whoops as we realized that two of the three bore our spaghetti tags. Rocky raced to the radio room for his identification sheets, and returned to announce that both *Peaches* and *Katie* were back. The third shark, also a female, was smaller than her companions—about nine-and-a-half feet—but she seemed, in chief diver Arrington's assessment, "feisty."

Our first goal was to tag the smallest shark, and I joined the cage team to watch as Blessington made several unsuccessful attempts through the open hatch on the roof of the cage. Finally, Marc pulled himself entirely through the hatch, bent far over the cage, stretched his long body to its limit, and as the shark

Rocky Strong injects a burst of shark repellent into the mouth of a great white. The chemical compound—sodium lauryl sulfate or SLS—proved successful in driving away all three great whites tested. The repelled sharks left the baited area and were not seen for many days afterward.

The tagging of great whites from Alcyone's swimstep required both concentration and quick reflexes. On occasion, a shark in pursuit of bait would lunge high enough to bite the step.

passed far below along the bottom of the cage, neatly affixed a tag. If there was a white shark tagging event in the Olympics, Blessington would be the odds-on favorite.

Though we were unaware at the time, our newcomer would eventually become almost a mascot to the expedition. By the time we completed our last voyage to Dangerous Reef, she had been sighted alongside *Alcyone* on 24 days during three different expeditions—a period spanning 580 days. During her first hours in our presence, she was named after Paul Martin's wife. While the original is a charming and gentle woman, our piscine *Rosy* was an out and out hazard. Once, while Chuck Davis was filming through an open cage door, *Rosy* tried to dash through the door and join the divers in the cage. Fortunately, Blessington alertly slid the door shut just in front of her snout. *Rosy* circled about and headed for the open filming slot. Whipping her tail, she forced her head almost all the way into the cage, a development watched with keen interest by Blessington and Davis.

We adjourned for a hurried lunch and returned to find all three sharks seemingly waiting for us, a happy turn of events. During our second dive, an incident transpired that would dominate mealtime conversations for a day or two.

We decided to lower the plastic cylinder into the midst of the sharks. Unfortunately, the only way to enter the cylinder is through the top. Since climbing into an eight-foot-high cylinder is awkward on the rear deck, we had followed an easier system. The cylinder was first lowered into position in the water, then chief diver Arrington swam down, opened the two top hatches, and squeezed in. It was a complicated maneuver, since the hatch openings were just wide enough to accomodate a diver with tanks. The entry required first passing under the bridle and the lines securing the cylinder.

When Arrington was ready to leap into the water, we carefully surveyed the area. None of the three sharks was visible. Unfortunately, we could not see down through the deck of the ship. Just as Arrington jumped, Bruno Gicquel spotted *Peaches* emerging from beneath *Alcyone*. Arrington heard Bruno yell "Shark!" just as his feet hit the water.

Beneath the surface, Arrington saw *Peaches* passing only ten feet away and faced a difficult decision. Should he keep his eyes on the shark or whip about and attempt to enter the cylinder quickly? Instinct told him to take the latter course. As he recalled afterward, turning his back on a fifteen-foot great white shark while swimming in a pool of blood was perhaps the hardest thing he had done in a lifetime of diving.

Arrington darted to the top of the cylinder, opened the hatches and plunged, but his regulator caught the rim of the huge tube and for a moment he hung motionless with his legs exposed. He pulled back, realigned himself and plunged again, this time dropping easily into the cylinder. To Arrington, unaware of the shark's movements and driven by a rush of adrenalin, the episode seemed endless. He later estimated that perhaps a minute had passed while he was working feverishly to free his tank and slip into the cylinder. Only months later, when we viewed film of the incident, did he learn how anxiety had seemed to expand the passage of time in his mind. The entire maneuver took only about three seconds. Through it all, as our film proved, *Peaches* showed no sign of interest in the silver-suited man.

Later in the dive, however, she did seem to grow curious about the human encased in plastic. From far below, she suddenly dashed upward, bumping her snout against the hollow plastic bars serving as a floor, bending them several inches apart through the force of her momentum, and startling Arrington.

Rosy returned to *Alcyone*'s stern several times during the next few days, enabling Rocky Strong to test a potential shark repellent he had carried aboard. Oddly enough, the chemical, known as sodium lauryl sulfate (SLS), is a common ingredient in hair shampoo. The process leading to its discovery had begun when noted shark specialist Dr. Eugenie Clark, a longtime friend who accompanied us on our first shark expeditions in the 1960s, found that a milky secretion from a Red Sea flatfish called the Moses sole seemed to fend off sharks effectively. Nature does not produce enough of the chemical to make it widely available, but researchers noticed that the secretion had surfactant properties similar to everyday detergents. Our old friend Don Nelson was one of the leaders in this research, undertaking field tests of several candidate compounds. He and

Rosy rises to glimpse activity on Alcyone's *stern. Unlike most shark species, great whites commonly raise their heads out of the water, presumably to view* surface objects. This may indicate that, like some fish, their eyes are especially adapted to accommodate to the different refraction qualities of air and water.

other researchers found that such surfactant compounds did, in fact, repel several species of sharks when the chemical was squirted directly in the mouth. Such tests on great white sharks, however, had never been attempted.

Using a syringe invented by Nelson—about the size of a small automatic rifle—Rocky positioned himself on the swimstep and waited cautiously for the opportunity to spray the harmless, soapy substance into *Rosy*'s mouth. Time after time, baits were jerked into the air near him as she lurched behind,

Jean-Michel and technician Eddie Paul discuss the fabrication of an artificial great white. By introducing a remote-controlled dummy among living sharks, Cousteau hoped to learn how whites might respond to encounters with others of their own kind.

mouth agape. After countless near misses, the shark emerged near Rocky's feet and he managed to propel a burst of the liquid between her teeth. The serving was equivalent to the contents of a soda can, and represented a solution of ten percent SLS cut with water. Immediately *Rosy* swung away from the ship and dashed out of sight. She did not return for several days. A similar test on another shark brought the same promising results.

The discovery of a practical shark repellent would ease the fears of millions of people the world over. It has long been a goal of shark researchers, whose work has received occasional surges of funding when shark-attack incidents have aroused the public. Interest in shark repellents probably peaked during World War II, when downed airmen and sailors faced the threat of sharks, particularly in the tropical Pacific. The pressure to develop a trustworthy repellent was so great that it prompted a memorable exchange in the British House of Commons. In answer to critics who charged the government's repellent research was insufficient, Winston Churchill responded preemptorily, "You may rest assured that the British Government is entirely opposed to sharks."

A repellent known as Shark Chaser—consisting of black dye and copper acetate in a small, water-soluble cake—was widely touted as an effective wartime defense against sharks, and it

perhaps boosted the morale of the thousands of servicemen who carried it. But it proved largely ineffective in tests conducted after the war.

Does the apparent effectiveness of SLS mean that humanity is finally on the verge of a reliable shark repellent? Yes and no. Well-equipped divers or occupants of a life raft might be able to inject the substance into the mouths of sharks that appear in full view, but a lone swimmer would be ill-prepared for such a task. It is unlikely that most swimmers would be armed with the necessary squirting device, or could carry enough of the chemical to use it repeatedly in the presence of several sharks. Swimmers might best be protected by a substance that could form a protective cloud about them. But tests have shown that such clouds produced by surfactants, which are quickly diluted and dispersed in the sea, are too weak to discourage sharks.

Shortly after our experiences with *Rosy*, another female arrived who seemed to embody all we had hoped to find in a great white shark. She was thirteen feet long, sleek, and beautiful. Filming her for hours underwater, Deloire was so taken with her elegant form and graceful motions that he insisted she be named *Isabelle,* after his wife. At his urging, we permitted a one-time diversion in our scientific program. Deloire was adamant that such natural perfection not be flawed by human intervention. There were some grumblings, but the will of the French artist prevailed. We left *Isabelle* untagged.

Yet *Isabelle* did provide us with some valuable scientific insights. The question often arose in our conversations aboard ship: how intelligent is the great white shark? With information about the creature so sparse and preliminary, such speculation bears little scientific merit. Yet it is human nature to wonder about the cleverness of other species. Is a horse or a pig more intelligent? A dolphin or an orca? In the matter of sharks, the age-old supposition is that they are not much more than hunger-driven bundles of muscles and reproductive gear. "The eyes were sightless in the black," wrote Peter Benchley in *Jaws,* "and the other senses transmitted nothing extraordinary to the small, primitive brain."

But many researchers now believe that most sharks, based on the ratio of brain size to bulk, may have as much intelligence as dogs or birds. Our interest was not so much in the appraisal of intelligence—a hopeless quest for the most part—but in the capacity of the great white shark to change its attack strategies to fit new circumstances. From such evidence as bite marks on pinnipeds and details of attacks on humans, some researchers theorize that great whites attack surreptitiously from below because they are too sluggish or dull to overcome agile prey species, such as sea lions, in any other way.

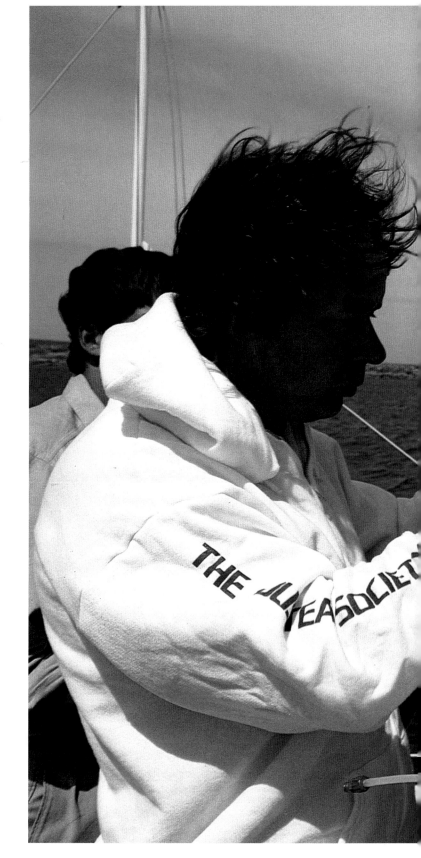

After shipment from Paul's California workshop to South Australia, the ten-foot-long artificial shark is assembled on Alcyone. From left: Eddie Paul, Capkin Van Alphen, and Marc Blessington.

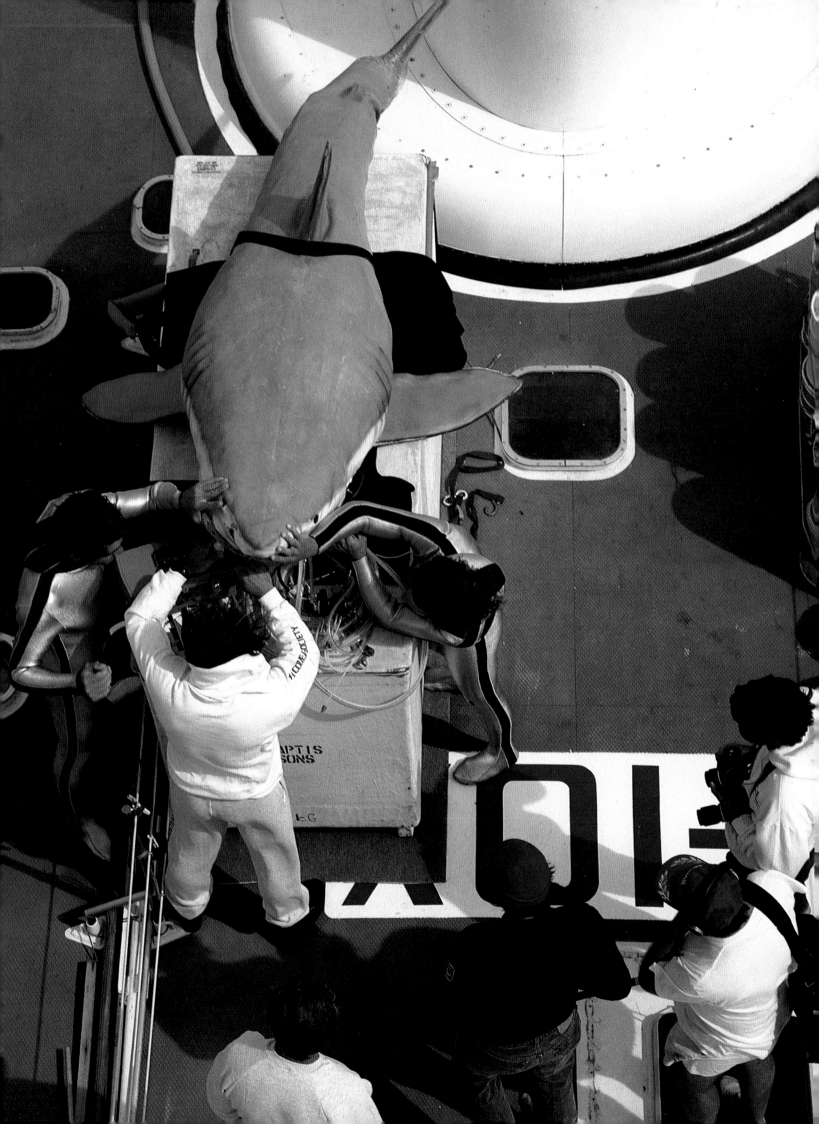

Throughout our expeditions, we had countless opportunities to observe sharks frustrated by our somewhat unorthodox baiting techniques, designed to bring them close for tagging. We forced them to work hard for a meal. In the process, some of the whites seemed not only persistent but armed with a repertoire of tricks. *Isabelle* was such a shark.

She proved to be as cagey as she was comely. During her first day alongside *Alcyone*, she experienced the same carrot-and-stick baiting game introduced to every shark. *Isabelle* persisted in the chase for a time. But in one instance, after rushing a tuna five or six times and failing to catch it as it was withdrawn, she altered her strategy. On her next approach she dashed at the bait quickly, then suddenly slowed down, as if uninterested. She coasted slowly to within five feet of it, banked slightly to the right as if to leave, glided four feet beyond the bait, and then WHAM! With lightning speed she whipped about and hit the tuna before Van Alphen could possibly reel it in. Apparently convinced of the success of her new tactic, *Isabelle* tried exactly the same maneuver three more times. Van Alphen, now ready for the trick, pulled the tuna away. *Isabelle* wasted no more time in this fruitless and inefficient pursuit. She left his bait station to try another.

We were greatly intrigued by another question about white shark behavior. Often, more than one shark and as many as six or seven, circled *Alcyone* to investigate the baits and the odor corridor. We wondered how the sharks regarded one another. Was there a social hierarchy among great whites? Few previous observers, and no prior scientific expedition, had been blessed with so many opportunites to witness their interactions. In an article published in the Cousteau Society's *Calypso Log* shortly after the second expedition, Rocky Strong described what we noted about the sharks' behavior:

They typically swam in opposite orbits, seeming to avoid one another while taking turns at the baits. When a new shark arrived, it naturally investigated the source of the overwhelming scent that had guided it for perhaps a couple of miles. With the arrival of a new shark, those already on the scene, apparently subdued by the lack of obtainable food, would suddenly express renewed interest. Along with the newcomer, they would make noticeably frequent approaches. Following this period of intense "claim-staking" activity, the largest shark present usually spent the most time near our baits.

Smaller sharks apparently deferred to bigger ones, but there were no firm rules. For example, sharks that had been around for several days and had fed, usually seemed less motivated. Newcomers that exhibited strong feeding drives were often tolerated even if they were smaller....

Social order could be maintained, but required constant "adjustments" to accomodate changing conditions. Only rarely was

fighting necessary. In light of the surprisingly complex social interactions we observed, labels like "mindless killers" no longer apply.

Months earlier, the question of how a white shark behaves toward another of its kind had so interested me that I set in motion plans for an unusual experiment. My idea had little to do with the traditional scientific program we were engaged in—tagging, tracking, repellent tests, and the like. The history of Cousteau expeditions is not only to gather such data, but to ask offbeat questions, sometimes crazy questions, and to attempt "experiments" that are out of the ordinary. Sometimes they prove worthless; sometimes they expand our horizons of perception by evoking further questions no one had thought to ask, which might in turn lead to more new questions and new knowledge.

I wanted to see what would happen if a real great white shark were confronted with an artificial great white shark. I wondered if the living shark might become aggressive. I wondered if it might attack a perceived foe of its own species. I wondered if its senses might identify the model shark as a fake, leading the real shark to be indifferent.

Before embarking on our second expedition, I had asked Californian Eddie Paul, who fashions special-effects devices for the movies, to build us a life-size model of a great white. Starting from scratch, Eddie created a ten-foot mechanical shark with a flexible, ribbed LEXAN frame covered by latex skin. Air lines from a single Scuba tank fed a pneumatic propulsion system, so that the shark's tail swept to and fro. The motion was not as smooth or powerful as that of a real shark, but we hoped the appearance would suffice in the low-visibility conditions undersea.

On February 26, still crated from its transpacific flight, the mechanical shark was carried aboard *Alcyone* and promptly dubbed *Allison*. For two days, we assembled and tested the buoyancy and swimming action of the model in the water. In the extremely murky conditions of the test site, where no cages were employed, the divers found themselves startled on occasion when *Allison*, looking like the real thing, suddenly emerged from the watery haze and headed in their direction.

On March 1, with *Rosy* and *Isabelle* present, we lowered the artificial shark and began our experiment. Deloire filmed from one cage while Eddie controlled the air lines that moved

Paul stretches the shark's latex skin over a skeleton composed of LEXAN, the same rigid plastic used in making the cylindrical dive cage. Paul named the artifical shark Allison, *purportedly after a former girlfriend.*

Allison's tail from another. Initially, we were disappointed. The real sharks showed little curiosity in the model.

Then, *Peaches* arrived. It was obvious immediately that she was more interested than the others in *Allison*, and she quickly began to swim close to the model. Deloire saw a change in *Peaches*'s behavior. "She seemed nervous," he later told us. "Several days earlier I had felt comfortable enough in her presence to step outside the cage to film her passes. But I wouldn't have done it today. Her comportment changed. To me, she looked dangerous."

Time after time *Peaches* passed near the smaller intruder, but she made no moves that could be interpreted as aggression. Eddie later told us that he felt when the model was immobile, *Peaches* approached more closely. Yet she did not attack.

On deck, Rocky and I speculated. While *Allison* may have appeared real at a distance, the intermittent tail movements and the posture of the model would probably have appeared abnormal to *Peaches*. Yet it is unlikely there were any stress-related activities conveyed to *Peaches'* senses, or any other signals indicating *Allison* was a living thing.

Perhaps she feared the model. Nearly all vertebrates behave cautiously at times, a survival characteristic that has served

From the protection of a shark cage, Paul (right) operates the pneumatic propulsion system installed in Allison. *Bursts of compressed air from a Scuba tank drive the tail from side to side, roughly mimicking the action of real great whites.*

RIGHT:
Before sailing for Dangerous Reef, the team tests the artificial shark in waters believed free of great whites. Umbilical tubes carry compressed air for the propulsion system, but can also be used to pump blood into the shark.

species well across eons. While it may be hard for us to empathize with such a formidable creature, there is no reason to believe that even great white sharks are not scared in unfamiliar circumstances.

It is entirely possible, if not probable, that fear is the reason more humans are not attacked by great whites. Certainly there are ample opportunities for whites to attack humans in populated swimming, diving, or surfing areas. Yet the incidents are extraordinarily rare. Rodney Fox told us of a fisherman friend who often pulled up whites in his nets only a half-mile off one of South Australia's most crowded beaches. Had the sharks been inclined to hunt for humans, they would have found their fill easily, yet they did not bother. Maybe they preferred their traditional prey. Or maybe the human activity along the shallows frightened them.

At this point, with *Peaches* seemingly puzzled by the mechanical shark, we decided to change the conditions. We began to pump blood into *Allison* through an umbilical tube alongside the air lines.

Whether *Peaches* had previously perceived the model as a real shark or not, and whatever her behaviorial inclination toward it—and even with a cloud of bait and blood enveloping the scene—the introduction of more blood leaking from the model may have overridden all other motivating factors. It seemed to take her to the threshold of attack. First, she bumped the model, nose-to-nose, and rubbed her snout very slowly down the left side of the model's snout, perhaps still trying to comprehend the nature of the presence in her midst. Two minutes passed as she withdrew and circled.

Then she attacked, not wildly but deliberately. She swam swiftly to the model and then slowly, and perhaps experimentally, bit into the right gill area and, with a few thrashes of her head, tore away a large hole in the latex skin. Then she withdrew again for about four minutes and made a second attack, this time striking behind the right pectoral fin. A

The moment of attack. After circling the artificial shark warily and bumping against it, the fifteen-foot female called Peaches *suddenly turned and rushed* Allison, *attacking the gill area. Half again as large as the model,* Peaches *may have attacked in a show of dominance.*

ABOVE:
Peaches *withdraws after inflicting what surely would have been a fatal blow to a real shark.*

88

minute later, her third attack struck the umbilical, severing the air hose supplying both buoyancy and tail movement, and the line feeding blood.

At that point, *Rosy* appeared and made two passes at *Allison.* *Peaches* returned quickly, moving in a manner that seemed calculated to drive the interloper away, and *Rosy* departed. To Rocky and Barry, this behavioral observation would prove the most important result of the entire episode. They were not surprised by the attack upon a bleeding model, but the driving away of a living shark fascinated them.

Ten minutes later *Peaches* attacked the head of the model, and five minutes after that made a fifth and very violent attack at the now-open right gills. Curiously, all five attacks had been to the right side of the model and were centralized around the gill region. As Rocky pointed out, the gills represent perhaps the easiest place on the shark's body to open an intrusive wound. Crabs invading the corpse of a dead shark in an aquarium enter through the gills or the cloaca.

By now *Allison* was badly damaged and the decision was made to haul her from the water. Inspecting the model on deck, we were astonished by the power of *Peaches'* bites. The LEXAN ribs, which were twice the thickness of the diving cylinder walls, had been shattered by the force of the bites.

Some four hours later, when the dive team made another descent, *Peaches* was still circling *Alcyone.*

In the aftermath of the model shark experiment, and with our second expedition drawing to a close, we were left with a host of questions. Did *Peaches* think she was attacking a real white shark, or did the blood overcome any inhibitions she might

The team witnessed five attacks by Peaches *on the artificial shark, each after about five minutes of circling. The bites snapped ribs made of bullet-proof plastic as if they were twigs. Interestingly, all attacks were to the right side, most concentrated around the vulnerable gills.*

have had—either out of fear or a revulsion against attacking her own species? Did the interval between attacks, approximately five minutes, imply confusion or perhaps the attraction-repulsion conflict that many animals experience when approaching others of the same species? Since the intensity of the attacks seemed to increase with time, was her cautious ambivalence gradually overcome as she became accustomed to the experience of attacking something that did not fight back? Did the fact that the ten-foot model was smaller suggest that *Peaches*—fifteen feet long—was behaving in a dominant role? After all, when *Rosy*—about the same size as the model—

entered the scene, she was seemingly driven away. What can we derive from the fact that *Peaches* was deeply interested in the model upon her arrival, while two smaller sharks, both of which had proven vigorous in their pursuit of baits, seemed disinterested? In that regard, I was interested in how our team often remarked that each shark seemed to have a different personality, some appearing calmer and slower, some more nervous and aggressive.

In the end, as we headed for Port Lincoln, we were left to ponder the one thing conclusively demonstrated by our

mechanical shark—the extraordinary power of a great white when it makes the decision to attack, whatever its target. Tied to our deck in full view of the bridge lay a nearly dismantled *Allison*, her metal and plastic viscera exposed to the salt air through gaping holes in her side. Watching shreds of latex flapping in the wind about cloven ribs of supposedly impenetrable plastic, I recalled the words of marine biologist Robin Milton Love. In the midst of a serious technical description of the great white shark, Love wrote: "When you have an animal that can munch on bat rays and elephant seals, you aren't talking chicken fat."

The dive team inspects the shattered remains of Allison. *From left: Strong, Van Alphen, and Paul. Behind them is Paul Martin, in the green shirt.*

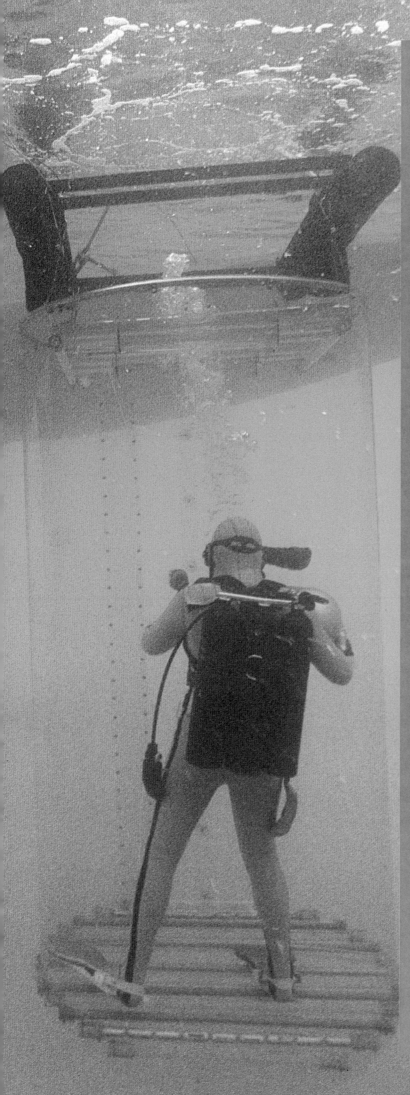

FOUR
THE MOST MISPER-CEIVED CREATURE ON EARTH

That which has always been accepted by everyone, everywhere, is almost certain to be false.
PAUL VALERY
Tel Quel

The worst of the austral winter seemed to be on the wane as we reconvened in Port Lincoln for Expedition Three. Watching Barry Bruce scurry back and forth loading an assortment of cases and crates aboard *Alcyone*, I realized that his scientific luggage was increasing with each voyage, and so was our research program. In the four-and-a-half months since our last mission to Dangerous Reef, the scientific team had decided to intensify efforts to track great white sharks. Attempting to follow an ingested pinger had proven very difficult during the first two expeditions, so Barry brought aboard several transmitters designed to be secured with harmless barbs to the exterior of a shark's body—basically the same technique that had succeeded so well with our spaghetti tags.

During the first expedition, we had decided not to employ our small inflatable rubber Zodiacs when great whites were present—a policy heartily endorsed by the crew, who had read the popular accounts of small boats bitten and sunk by white sharks. Accordingly, Barry also brought to the Port Lincoln wharf an eighteen-foot aluminum boat furnished as a tracking vessel by the South Australian Department of Fisheries. When the time for departure came, someone aboard *Alcyone* noticed a pool of water in the bottom of the new vessel. Efforts to find the leak failed, and since there was no alternative but to use the aluminum boat, we set out for Dangerous Reef towing a vessel that was slowly sinking. Though the leak was too small to pose any great danger, it would mean that tracking teams would be

As the ghostly image of an approaching white emerges from the haze, another shark seems curious to inspect Alcyone's hull. Occasionally rubbing against the vessel, some sharks inadvertently decorated themselves with splotches of the ship's white paint. (Sharp scales called dermal denticles give shark skin a sandpaper roughness.)

To learn more about the movement habits of great white sharks, the Cousteau team began an unprecedented series of trackings, using ultrasonic transmitters temporarily fixed to the backs of sharks. Barry Bruce (center), monitors pings emitted from a shark-borne transmitter, while Andrew Fox (left) records the map coordinates. Rock; Strong steers the launch and takes bearings with a hand compass.

forced to bail water occasionally as they followed the sea's most formidable shark at close range. Mindful of the dark humor in the situation, some wag aboard *Alcyone* christened the tracking boat with a name that stuck—*Titanic*.

Late in the afternoon of August 1, under a cerulean sky and across smooth seas, we set out for Dangerous Reef. But for two significant newcomers, the crew was unchanged from the last expedition. Christophe Jouet-Pastre, an experienced French navy captain, had come aboard to take the helm, replacing Nicholas Dourassoff. Dr. John Stevens had joined the scientific team while Rocky Strong fulfilled other committments. A senior biologist at Tasmania's CSIRO Marine Laboratories, Stevens is one of the world's leading shark specialists, and a forceful voice on behalf of shark conservation.

When the anchor was secured, and the evening meal underway, Barry and John began establishing our blood corridor once again. The tommy roughs arrived promptly, adding silver flashes to a kaleidoscopic twilight scene that included a cobalt-blue sea flushed with red clouds of blood and a western horizon fading through pink hues to purples. Within an hour, the southern cross would appear as a reminder to most of us that we were visiting a foreign hemisphere.

At 5:00 A.M., while making rounds of the ship during his watch, engineer Patrick Allioux noticed a tuna bait missing from one of the lines adrift at the stern. Ever polite, Patrick avoided waking the entire crew by ringing the dinner bell to announce the presence of a shark. Instead, he roused Barry Bruce and the two sat on the rear storage bin staring at the pool of water lit by the stern spotlights, both hunched over against a chill morning breeze. Finally, a dorsal fin broke the water and Barry wrote in his notebook that our twenty-second shark had arrived. In honor of the vessel's new captain, the ten-foot male was named *Chris*.

As Patrick coaxed the new shark near the swimstep with horsemeat on a line, Barry quickly stuck a blue and yellow spaghetti tag into the skin along its back. As the crew came on deck one by one, each took a turn with the bait lines. Barry had anticipated a long wait for a tracking candidate, but *Chris's* aggressive pursuit of bait indicated he was likely to remain by the ship long enough for a tracking operation to be organized.

By now, each crew member knew just what had to be done. Once a transmitter had been successfully attached to a shark, all chumming would cease, so that our influence over the creature's behavior would be minimized. Our most experienced sailors—Captain Jouet-Pastre, Thierry Stern, and Paul Martin—would be on wheel watch aboard *Alcyone*. They would follow the tracking boat by naked eye or radar at an optimum range of about half a mile, trying not to approach closer than half that distance. At fifteen-minute intervals, they would record *Alcyone's* coordinates, the range and bearing of the tracking boat, and the bottom depth. Each hour they would note as well the wind speed and direction, the temperature, the state of the sea, and the light conditions in the sky.

The rest of the crew would rotate through four-hour shifts of three men aboard the tracking vessel. One man would drive the boat, another would operate the receiver and a hand-bearing compass to keep track of the shark, while the third recorded the animal's range, bearing, and depth as they were called out every fifteen minutes. Occasionally, the depth would be noted at fifteen-second intervals over a five-minute period, giving greater detail to the shark's vertical movements.

As the team knew, the most important—and hardest—thing about tracking animals is positioning oneself close enough to maintain contact without chasing the animal, thus altering its natural movements. Concentration would be essential.

At about 9:00 A.M., Barry managed to implant a transmitter on *Chris's* side just aft of the gills. Chumming ceased and the first tracking team set out in *Titanic* armed not only with their scientific pursuit gear but a supply of sunscreen, sandwiches, and soda.

A half hour after the baiting ended, *Chris* veered away from *Alcyone* but remained close to Dangerous Reef. For two hours, he circled the reef slowly in an expanding clockwise arc. By mid-afternoon, he was four miles west of the reef. As the sun was setting, he returned in a nearly direct line to the shallows around Dangerous Reef, swimming parallel to shore. If *Chris* was hoping to surprise a sea lion in the dusk, he was following a reasonable strategy. There was no indication he succeeded, however, if in fact this was his purpose.

With the sun almost gone, we temporarily lost track of the shark as it passed close to shore. Suddenly, the pings of the transmitter were drowned out by a clatter of crab and shrimp sounds. The team circled the island for nearly an hour before picking up the pings again as *Chris* was departing Dangerous Reef for open water. During the next hour, he swam southward about two miles, then turned eastward.

Forty-five minutes later, about four miles from Dangerous Reef, a school of common dolphins descended on the tracking boat. Their chatter completely overwhelmed the pinging sounds, and they continued to squeal into the receiver for two hours. All hope of reestablishing contact with *Chris* was lost. The entire tracking had lasted slightly more than thirteen hours. Barry Bruce, who was acting as the tracker, had to remove the headphones periodically because the volume of the dolphins' vocalizations became painful to his ears. At times, the team watched the exuberant mammals chattering directly into the transponder head from only six inches away.

"One prepares for all sorts of eventualities," Barry said as he climbed back aboard *Alcyone*. "We expect the equipment to fail or the transmitter to fall from the shark. We do not anticipate that our work will be defeated by an undersea choir performing as if they were in a talent contest."

Actually, there had been another unanticipated development during a tracking mission on the previous expedition. The incident occurred on one of our unsuccessful attempts to follow a shark bearing a swallowed transmitter. Andrew Fox, Rodney's son, had joined *Alcyone's* team for a time, and this night he was operating the receiver aboard the tracking boat. The job demands absolute attention. One listens intently through headphones for the pinging signal while bent over the gunwhale with an arm outstretched to hold a spear-like rod, at the bottom of which the transponder is kept submerged. Though the tracker is often leaning near the sea surface, there is little danger since he is constantly aware of the shark's whereabouts.

This night, however, a second shark had apparently become curious about the little boat moving along the water ceiling and had risen to the surface to investigate. As Andrew bent toward the surface in rapt concentration, kneeling in the bottom of the

tracking boat, the snout of this second great white shark suddenly erupted from the black water only a yard from his head. Andrew is a young man, still limber enough to leap to his feet in a microsecond of terror, and he did so. Perhaps the commotion and the shouts gave the shark pause. He drifted back downward and did not return.

As *Chris* was departing a weather front was arriving, and the seas rose steadily during the next two days. Nevertheless, we welcomed two returnees to our stern on August 3. *Rosy*, who had served as our first repellent-test subject during the last expedition and who had been chased from the artificial shark by *Peaches*, appeared about breakfast time. She was followed fifteen minutes later by *Marc*, a 10-foot male tagged on the last day of the previous mission.

We briefly discussed the possibility of tracking one of the sharks, but dismissed the notion as too dangerous. A tracking team braving choppy seas to pursue a shark could find themselves quickly swamped. We managed to lower Chuck Davis for a short still-photo dive. He reported the visibility at less than thirty feet and the ride in the cage something akin to torture. By 2:00 P.M. we had weighed anchor and were escaping the unworkable sea conditions for Port Lincoln.

While tracking teams trailed sharks in an aluminum launch, observers followed on Alcyone. *Precise records of each shark's route were kept by monitoring the launch through shipboard radar.*

RIGHT:
Charts of white-shark trackings revealed two characteristic horizontal movements. Cousteau scientists termed the pattern shown in red "island patrolling." There, the shark appeared to remain in the vicinity of a single island, as if maintaining a home range. The black line represents "interisland cruising," in which a shark traveled across a broader area, making sorties toward islands encountered along the way. Presumably, this was to search for potential prey such as pinnipeds. Each tracking began with a third pattern, "downstream circling," which appeared to be a direct response to the chumming. The team theorized that the sharks were consistently and persistently following bait particles drifting downstream, before taking up the patrolling or cruising patterns.

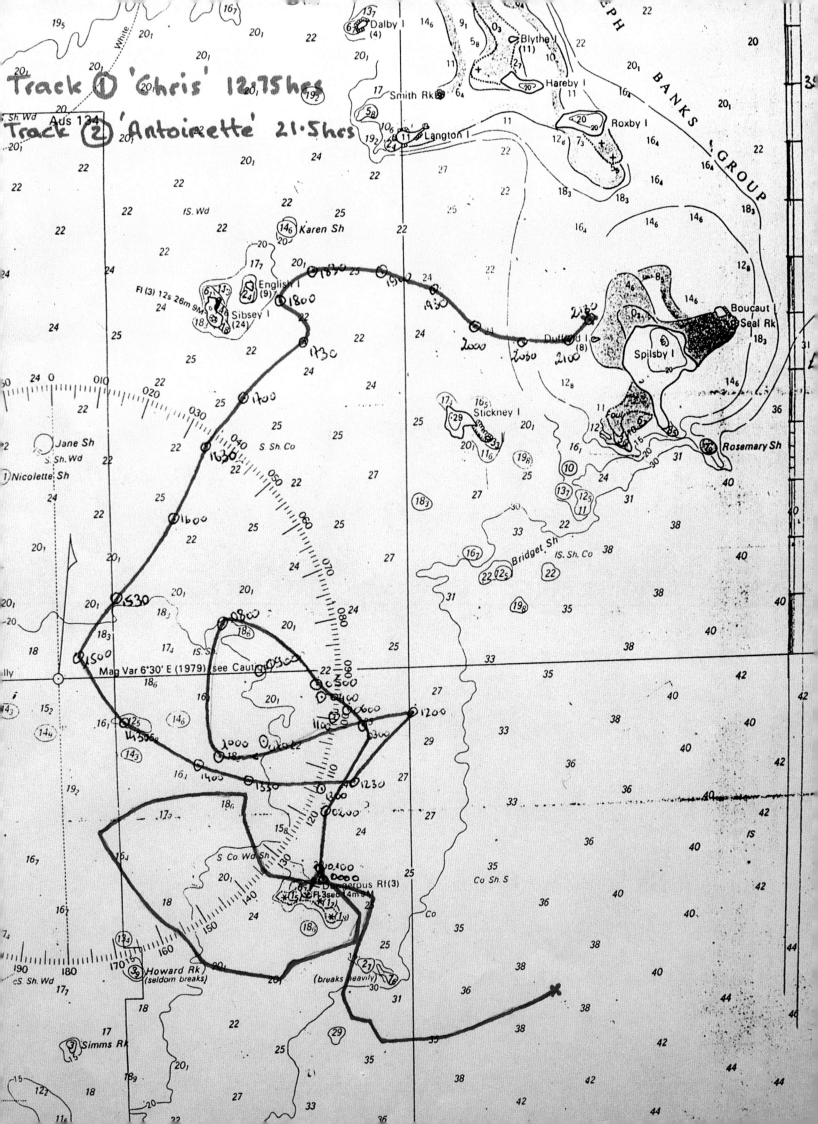

Gale-force winds kept us docked for three days, and when we returned to Dangerous Reef, *Rosy* was again the first shark to appear at *Alcyone*'s stern. Whether or not other great white sharks were permanent residents of the waters around this tiny island was unclear but we were beginning to suspect that *Rosy* did not wander far from the area.

For Paul Martin, whose wife was the original Rosy, the return of her namesake was cause for the kind of elaborate greetings one reserves for a long-lost pet. But for Barry Bruce, whose steady demeanor befits the noble cause of science, *Rosy* was merely an available representative of her kind. Her appearance offered the opportunity he had been awaiting to open a new theater of great white shark research.

Accordingly, with the sea now glassy and *Rosy* hanging about our bait lines, Barry arrived on deck with a biopsy needle. Lying prone on the swimstep while the team lured the shark near with the bait lines, he reached out swiftly on one of *Rosy*'s passes and withdrew a plug of flesh from her back with the needle. To a casual visitor, the maneuver might have appeared supremely courageous or foolhardy. But by now we were so accustomed to being in close proximity to great whites that no one aboard was much impressed by Barry's boldness.

The tissue sample was quickly transferred to a sealed glass bottle and frozen in liquid nitrogen, kept at a temperature of minus 190 degrees Fahrenheit in a special container. Barry's hope was to accumulate several tissue samples and then to subject them to mitochondrial DNA electrophoresis—a process that identifies distinctive genetic traits. Such laboratory work may provide clues as to whether South Australian great whites form sub-populations that do not interbreed. This kind of information is critical to wildlife managers like Barry, since many small populations require a very different management strategy than does a single, large, interbreeding population. In the future, as great white shark research expands in other parts of the world, the tissue samples could also be compared to those of distant populations, giving science a better understanding of relationships among the species as a whole.

Two more days of bad weather buffeted *Alcyone*, forcing us to shift our anchorage around Dangerous Reef several times to ride out changing wind and swell directions. The frustration in this was not so much the bother of moving but the abandonment of a bait corridor with each move. Our experience to date also lent some credence to Rodney Fox's contention that great

Barry Bruce seems to mirror the countenance of an arriving great white as he prepares to take a flesh sample.

whites avoid the surface during rough weather. It was not always so, but, to borrow an old punch line, that was the way to bet.

Nevertheless, despite the large seas, three sharks appeared at the stern late in the afternoon of August 9. The first was the largest shark we had yet observed on the expedition, a fourteen-foot female we named *Antoinette* after our hardworking assistant cameraman, Antoine Rosset. (The preponderance of females at Dangerous Reef was complicating our desire to honor each crewman. Antoine shrugged characteristically, as if to acknowledge that an honor was an honor no matter the gender.)

In fact, we had identified two previous fourteen-foot sharks during the second expedition, but *Antoinette* was markedly larger of girth than the others, leading us to wonder what kind of genetic or environmental factors might produce such a dramatic difference in sharks of the same length, or if *Antoinette* was pregnant. Though Chuck Davis and Ian Chapman, coordinator of logistics for most of our Australian trips and a superb diver, were able to descend long enough to take still photos of *Antoinette*, the seas were too turbulent to attempt either underwater moviemaking or a sonic tracking.

Soon *Antoinette* was joined at the stern by the inveterate *Rosy* and a new eleven-foot female who was dubbed *Amy*. All three remained near us through the evening, and gradually the rough seas subsided enough to make possible another tracking operation. Just before midnight, Barry implanted a sonic transmitter along *Antoinette*'s back and our second chase ensued. *Antoinette*'s nighttime wanderings immediately proved more erratic than had *Chris*'s. With the cessation of chumming, she headed about three miles north of Dangerous Reef, then wandered for about twelve hours in a generally clockwise circle over an open-sea area three miles across. About an hour later she set off in a winding northerly arc of about twenty-five miles that took her near Sibsey and English Islands, then eastward to Spilsby Island. Where *Chris*'s movements had seemed to represent a kind of island patrolling around Dangerous Reef, at least during our tracking, *Antoinette*'s more linear path, with occasional sorties toward islands, seemed more like interisland cruising.

As *Antoinette* made her way toward Spilsby, the winds increased to 20 knots, gusting to 25, and soon the tracking boat was negotiating perilous seas. *Titanic* was plunging into the waves and taking water over the bow. When *Antoinette* swam into the shallows along tiny Duffield Island, north of Spilsby, the team lost contact with her. Searching about for the shark's signal would have meant further endangering the storm-tossed team, so Captain Jouet-Pastre ordered the tracking terminated. The pursuit had lasted nearly 22 hours and covered about 36 miles.

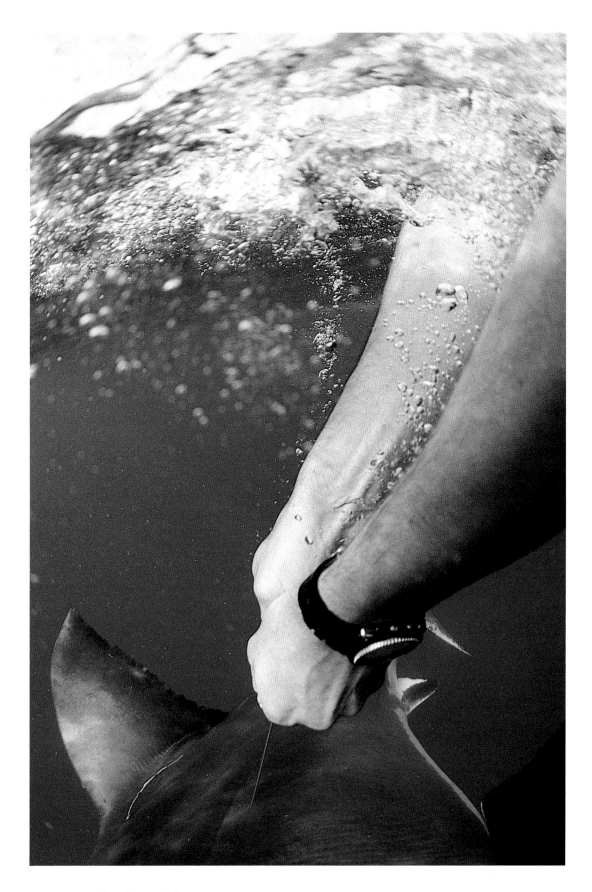

ABOVE AND RIGHT:

Capkin Van Alphen inserts a
biopsy needle into the back of
Donna Marie *as the twelve-foot
female passes* Alcyone's *stern.*
Van Alphen *withdraws quickly in
the event the shark should react*

to the needle. Generally, great
whites seemed little bothered by
such samplings or by the
implanting of fisheries tags. Here,
Donna Marie *simply cruised on
without visible response.*

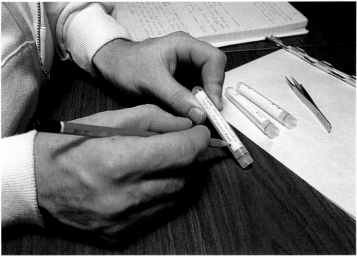

Plugs of tissue taken with the biopsy needle were stored in containers, then frozen for future DNA analysis. It is hoped that the tissue samples will help researchers determine if South

Australia's great whites constitute a distinct subpopulation, and to what extent white sharks here are related to those in other parts of the world.

During the week that followed our encounter with *Antoinette*, the weather became miserable. We returned to Port Lincoln for three days, then moved to Dangerous Reef, where we lasted only two days before heading back to the mainland. The brief interlude at Dangerous Reef was memorable only for the arrival of a shark so aggressive that even the normally unflappable Barry Bruce termed it a "mean" shark. Though he was able to tag the ten-foot female, and to name her *Patricia*, he was astonished at the shark's ability to steal bait before the crew could pull in the lines. After consuming four tuna heads, *Patricia* disappeared.

Finally, with no signs that the storm would abate and winds increasing to forty knots, we gave up and sought safe harbor in Port Lincoln. In the Port Lincoln Tavern that night, while the younger crew members mingled with the locals, a humorous remark by Paul Martin led our two scientists into a long discussion of great white shark reproduction. What Paul said, with his inimitable boyish charm and thick French accent, was that the great white males seemed to have "two zee-zees." Bruce and Stevens turned blank faces toward me, and I explained that this was the common French euphemism for male organs.

Well, corrected Barry amid a chorus of chuckles, they were not really *penises* but sausagelike, cartilage-supported extensions of the male's pelvic fins called "claspers." Still, in truth, they seemed to serve a similar function, at least in the few shark species where mating had been observed. During copulation a male shark grasped the pectoral fins or the back of a female with his teeth, then inserted one of his claspers into her cloaca. Sperm mixed with seawater ran down a furrow in the clasper and into her body. The term clasper was, in fact, a lucky misnomer attributed to Aristotle, who was the first observer to report the appendages and who believed they were used simply to embrace and hold a female. In fact, during copulation, a spine at the tip of the clasper flares out, snagging the uterine wall and locking the clasper in place.

Interestingly, few people had actually observed sharks copulating—among them our old friend Don Nelson, who had witnessed in the South Pacific the mating of both blacktip reef sharks (*Carcharhinus melanopterus*) and reef whitetips (*Triaenodon obesus*). And *no one* had ever been present at the mating of great white sharks. In fact, said Barry, virtually nothing was known for certain about any aspect of great white reproduction.

There had been a few unsubstantiated accounts of pregnant white sharks caught by fishermen, who estimated litter sizes of nine to eleven pups. And there was a documented account by a scientist who saw two adult females hauled aboard a Japanese

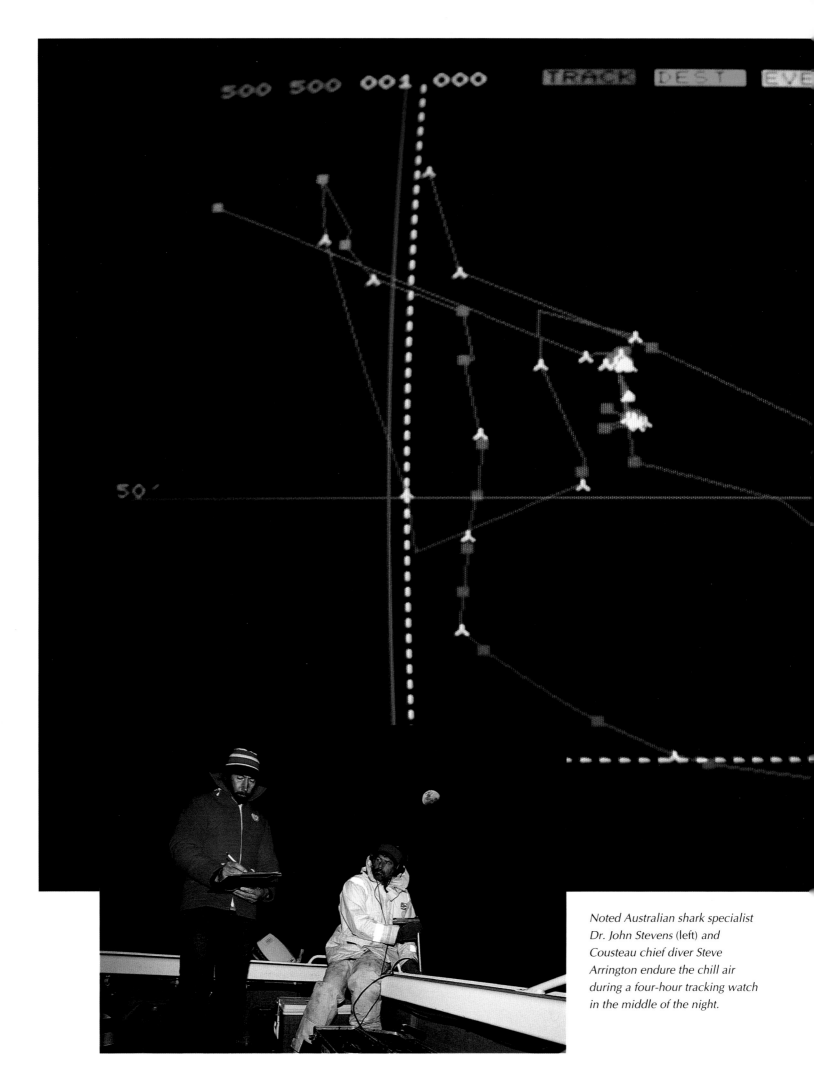

Noted Australian shark specialist Dr. John Stevens (left) and Cousteau chief diver Steve Arrington endure the chill air during a four-hour tracking watch in the middle of the night.

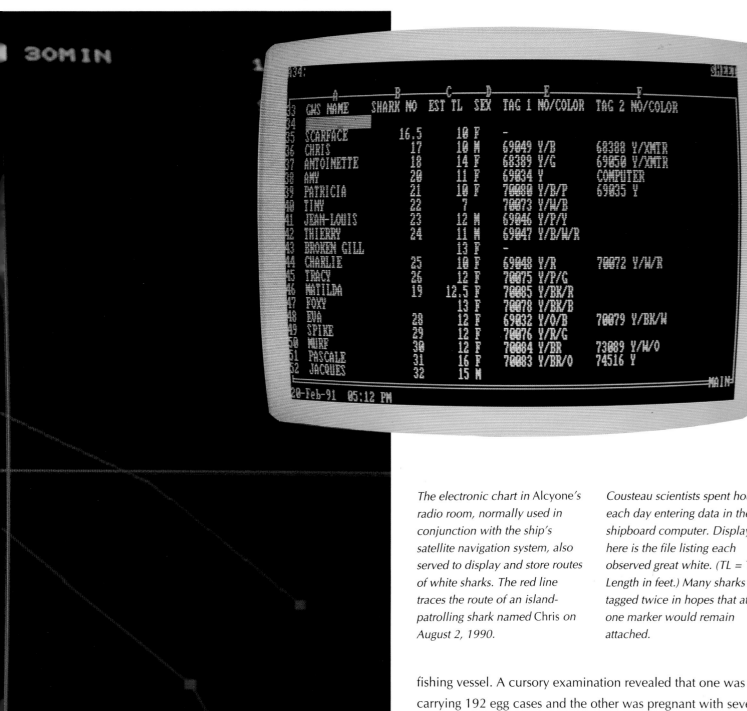

	GWS NAME	SHARK NO	EST TL	SEX	TAG 1 NO/COLOR	TAG 2 NO/COLOR
	SCARFACE	16.5	10	F	-	
	CHRIS	17	10	M	69049 Y/B	68300 Y/XMTR
	ANTOINETTE	18	14	F	68389 Y/G	69050 Y/XMTR
	AMY	20	11	F	69034 Y	COMPUTER
	PATRICIA	21	10	F	70000 Y/B/P	69035 Y
	TINY	22	7		70073 Y/W/B	
	JEAN-LOUIS	23	12	M	69046 Y/P/Y	
	THIERRY	24	11	M	69047 Y/B/W/R	
	BROKEN GILL		13	F	-	
	CHARLIE	25	10	F	69048 Y/R	70072 Y/W/R
	TRACY	26	12	F	70075 Y/P/G	
	MATILDA	19	12.5	F	70085 Y/BK/R	
	FOXY		13	F	70078 Y/BK/B	
	EVA	28	12	F	69032 Y/O/B	70079 Y/BK/W
	SPIKE	29	12	F	70076 Y/R/G	
	MURF	30	12	F	70084 Y/BR	73089 Y/W/O
	PASCALE	31	16	F	70083 Y/BR/O	74516 Y
	JACQUES	32	15	M		

20-Feb-91   05:12 PM

The electronic chart in Alcyone's *radio room, normally used in conjunction with the ship's satellite navigation system, also served to display and store routes of white sharks. The red line traces the route of an island-patrolling shark named* Chris *on August 2, 1990.*

Cousteau scientists spent hours each day entering data in the shipboard computer. Displayed here is the file listing each observed great white. (TL = Total Length in feet.) Many sharks were tagged twice in hopes that at least one marker would remain attached.

fishing vessel. A cursory examination revealed that one was carrying 192 egg cases and the other was pregnant with seven seemingly near-term embryos. Unfortunately, the embryos were discarded without accurate measurements being taken; however, photographs suggest they were about a meter in length. Since that is about the same size as the smallest free-swimming great whites reported in the scientific literature, both Barry and John believed it was reasonable to assume that great white pups started life already about a meter long.

From birth onward, Barry said, it is generally thought that great whites grow about a foot each year, that males reach maturity when they are about ten feet long and females when they are about thirteen to fourteen feet long. Barry himself had examined ten captured females in South Australia. In two of the sharks—an eight-footer and a thirteen-and-a-half footer—a hymen covered the vaginal opening, indicating they were still virgins.

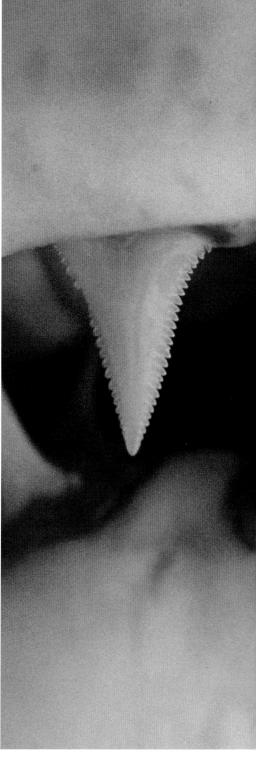

Two whites maintain a comfortable distance from one another—keeping their "personal space" as the crew called the behavior—while they circle at the stern of Alcyone. The smaller shark at the top appears about to turn away, maneuvering to avoid crossing the orbit of the larger shark. Note the elongated claspers extending behind the pelvic fins of each, clearly identifying them as mature males.

RIGHT:

The mouth of a juvenile white shark reveals how the form and function of their teeth change as the animals mature. The narrower teeth of young sharks, like these, are useful in grasping the fish and other elusive prey they feed upon, while the wider, stronger teeth of adults enable them to puncture the thick skins of marine mammals.

His examinations led Barry to conclude that great white reproduction follows the course of certain other sharks. That is, the young hatch, develop, and are nourished through a placenta within the mother, then are released through live birth into the wild. But for their size, they seem exact replicas of the adults from their first moment of life.

Except that the young receive no parental care, I remarked, the system does not seem radically different from our own human reproductive process. Barry nodded, and I took it a step further. Whereas some carnivores produce cuddly young that inspire human affection—such as with lion or tiger cubs, or

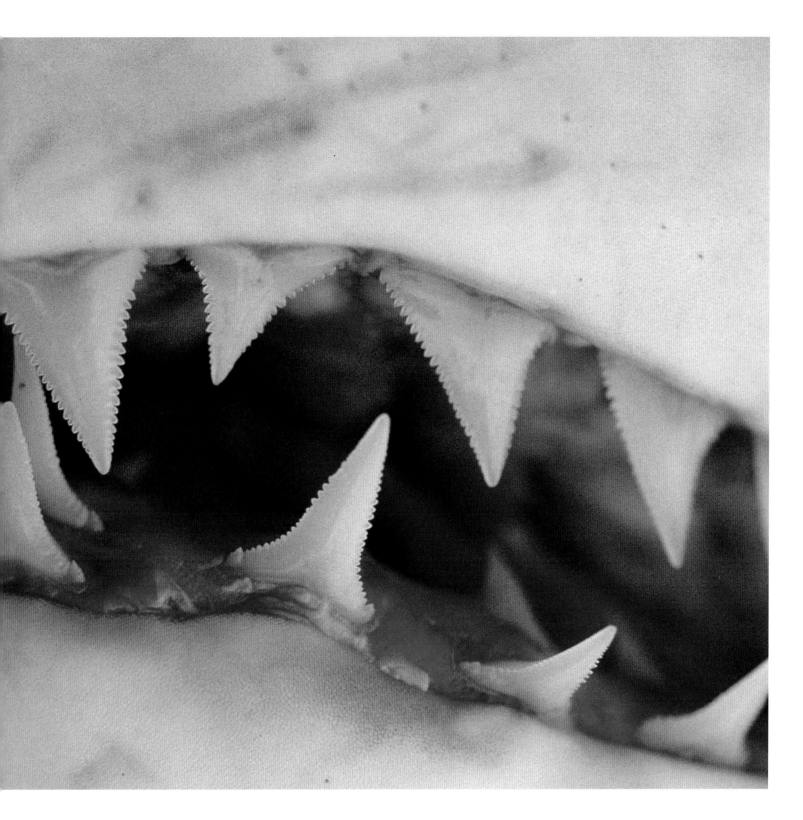

wolf pups—the poor shark never elicits our sympathy, even at birth, because it comes into the world looking like a shark.

Barry agreed, but he cautioned me not to extend a surfeit of pity toward the newborn great whites. The enormous number of egg cases reported in pregnant mothers also suggested that white shark reproduction was *oophagous*—an arcane term meaning that the embryos were cannibals. Like the embryos of other lamniform sharks, the family to which great whites belong, the first hatchlings within the uterus of a great white female probably supplement their nourishment by eating other embryos and the unfertilized eggs that continue to descend

during pregnancy. Thus eggs numbering in the hundreds may be pared down through cannabilism to a dozen or so survivors which comprise the birth litter.

As it happened, Barry knew of a Port Lincoln fisherman who had caught pregnant great whites, and since the weather made it impossible for us to return to sea, we sought him out the next day. Ted Monaghan had been fishing the waters of South Australia since the late fifties, principally setting nets for small commercial shark species, such as school sharks (*Galeorhinus galeus*) and gummy sharks (*Mustelus antarcticus*). In the course of his thirty years of fishing, Monaghan had caught two male

great white sharks in his nets and six females, three of which were pregnant.

Like most independent commercial fishermen, Monaghan had a profound curiosity about the marine world that provided him with the means to live, and he had a good memory. To test his credibility in a friendly way, John Stevens asked Monaghan several detailed questions about the reproductive systems of other shark species caught incidentally in his nets. The fisherman's accurate answers convinced Bruce and Stevens that he was both credible and serious.

One of the pregnant sharks pulled in by Monaghan was nearly fourteen feet long and carried eleven pups, two of which fell into the water while the shark was being hauled in. Of the remaining nine, one died on deck and the others were tossed back into the water. Monaghan estimated their length at about two feet.

He recalled that a seventeen-foot mother carried six or seven embryos a foot long, each connected to separate umbilical cords, which, when untwisted, stretched ten feet across the deck. Each umbilical cord was attached to a yellow yolk sac about the size of a softball. The third pregnant great white, which was about fifteen feet long, contained thirteen embryos, each only a couple inches in length.

Remarkably, between the simple discussion the evening before and the limited experiences of a single fisherman, we had just about covered all that is known about the procreation of the great white shark. Most of the public, I suspect, assumes that marine scientists possess detailed information about such a vital aspect of the world's most renowned shark. In fact, science knows painfully little about great whites because of the enormous logistical barriers to studying them, and the popular sources that supply the public with a broad impression of the animal are mostly dubious.

I wonder if there is another creature on earth so misperceived. We believe that great white sharks are primitive; but they are probably more recent to the planet than horses or whales. Their bodies are masterful models of evolutionary advancements and their reproductive systems bear some similarities to our own. We believe them to be no more than "swimming noses," yet they employ a battery of highly developed sense-detection systems, including the most sophisticated electrosensory system in the entire animal

Most great whites approached the dive cages warily. The Cousteau team believed the animals were probably confused by the puzzling circumstances: blood-saturated waters suggested abundant food, but only a few edible bait chunks floated among a baffling array of unfamiliar phenomena—including cages, divers, bubbles, and engine noises.

kingdom. We think of them as mindless killers, but they seem to exhibit complex social interactions. We believe that they are cold-blooded fish, but that they maintain body temperatures several degrees warmer than the surrounding water. We believe they are wildly ferocious, though they appear not only cautious to a high degree in unfamiliar circumstances but perhaps even scared on occasion.

Some might wonder why the reproductive strategy of a species like the great white should concern us. The answer involves another surprising aspect of the creature. Its mode of reproduction is one of several characteristics that make great whites, for all their might, highly vulnerable to depletion as a species. For eons they thrived, adapting as necessary to gradual changes in their environments. Though they grew slowly and produced relatively few (but well-developed) young, compared to most bony fishes they survived in the absence of any formidable ocean enemies. Suddenly, with the technological expansions of human fishing, the conditions have changed for great whites. They are threatened, as are many other species, with the possibility of being unable to replace themselves fast enough to avoid extinction. If they are not in fact endangered now, it seems an inevitability if commercial and sport fisheries continue their present growth. Limited by their low fecundity, great whites—and most other sharks—cannot make the quick comebacks possible among fishes that grow more rapidly and lay thousands of eggs to permit at least a few individuals to survive. Ironically, as Rocky Strong once put it, the great white shark's advanced reproductive system has become a kind of enemy within.

OPPOSITE:

The tendency of great whites to avoid close proximity to one another posed a risk for divers, who found it difficult to keep track of more than one shark at a time. While Deloire trains his camera through an open hatch on a shark to his left, an unseen shark appears behind him.

Though great whites inevitably rose, like this shark, to take surface baits, most did so after long periods of circling the area, sometimes for hours. The Cousteau team believes great whites are at least cautious toward the unfamiliar, long-limbed, alert and responsive animal that is a human—a possible explanation for the scarcity of their attacks on swimmers.

With the arrival of a high-pressure front on August 16, we raced back to Dangerous Reef, where sharks began to arrive only four hours after we started chumming. By day's end, we had tagged four new great whites. Barry and John were most intrigued by a fast-swimming seven-footer, appropriately christened *Tiny*. Barry reasoned that the youngster might one day furnish important data on the growth rates of great whites if it were seen again in the future.

That led Deloire to ask an obvious question: how long do great white sharks live? The general assumption among researchers, Barry said, is that they can live as long as twenty-five or thirty years. The evidence comes from examinations of captured specimens. Like other sharks, great whites carry a kind of diary within their bodies. A cross section of their cartilaginous backbones reveals growth rings like those of a tree. Calibrating this vertebral banding enables scientists to estimate the longevity of sharks in the wild. In contrast to the lifespan of the great white, the spiny dogfish (*Squalus acanthias*) is believed to live 65 to 70 years, and perhaps as long as 100. The significance of this shark, which reaches a length of only about five feet and is probably the most common shark species in the world, far outshines its rather mundane name. Because of

its abundance and its importance in commercial fisheries—twenty-seven million were taken annually off the Massachusetts coast at the turn of the century—the spiny dogfish has been studied more than any other shark. The unfortunate result is a tendency in the media to assume that all sharks are alike and what they are like is the spiny dogfish.

The next morning we found ourselves in the midst of a shark circus. Within three hours, seven great whites had come to investigate our blood and bait offerings. The four sharks from the previous day had returned, along with two new sharks and ever-reliable *Rosy*. During a thrilling dive, Deloire managed to film the shark assembly, which sometimes outnumbered the divers. To the eventual chagrin of our film editor in Los Angeles, David Saxon, the wary visitors kept enough distance from each other to defeat Deloire's attempts to capture them all dramatically in a single shot. Barry Bruce, on the other hand, obtained tissue samples from two of the sharks and succeeded in tagging all of them.

The dive team reported that these great whites seemed noticeably more aggressive than any previously observed. Though it was impossible to know the cause for certain, we wondered if the presence of so many in one place intensified the competition for our limited food offerings or heightened the expectations of proximity to a large food source. Perhaps the unusual situation simply made them nervous, or perhaps the turbulent seas of the past week or so had interfered with their hunting and made them hungrier than usual.

Whatever sparked the aggressiveness, it forced the dive team to new levels of alertness. Often, the sharks accelerated like jet liners on takeoff as they made runs between the two cages, which were about fifteen feet apart. Several times both Deloire and Davis had to fend off charging sharks with their cameras to keep them from barreling through open cage doors. Once, with his cage at the surface, Arrington stretched his body through the open top hatch to pass a camera to the deck crew. Suddenly, Davis grabbed the chief diver's ankles and jerked him back into the cage as a great white lurched his way. From underwater, the two men peered into a gaping mouth from only a foot away. Thin light shafts passing through the gill slits illuminated a tiny creature, which they believed to be a spider crab, walking along the roof of the shark's mouth.

We noticed something else among the sharks present this day. Several were badly scarred. The upper lobe of the tail was missing from a ten-foot female. Another female of about the same length was missing parts of both the upper and lower tail lobes. A thirteen-foot female, whom we named *Broken Gill*, had badly mangled gill slits on her right side. We had earlier noticed that *Rosy*, too, sported small scars along her head and just forward of her tail.

While some of the scars probably resulted from rough treatment by males during courtship, and *Rosy*'s in particular looked like scratch marks applied by a struggling pinniped, an alarming number of the wounds were of a nature to suggest the animals had come in contact with fishing gear. This theory gained credence when a twelve-foot female appeared bearing two hooks still embedded in her belly and a six-foot leader dangling from her jaws. The gear was clearly ripped from a commercial long-line, not from a gamefishing rig.

During one dive, Capkin noticed something that left us shaking our heads. While *Rosy* passed close to his cage, he caught sight of a fresh wound midway along the right side of her body. Others confirmed this on subsequent dives. The injury was perfectly circular, with a slight puckering along the edges. It was about a half-inch in diameter, and all who saw it agreed that it looked exactly like a bullet hole.

The following day our run of sharks continued, with another four circling about continuously. The day was memorable to the crew chiefly because it was their privilege to introduce a good-

As it courses slowly between steel and plastic dive cages, this great white employs a battery of senses to identify what is in its midst. Much of a shark's sensory perception system is still a mystery. For example, tiny pits on the tail are believed by some scientists to house olfactory organs—meaning that to some extent sharks may smell with their tails.

OVERLEAF:

A Cousteau diver reaches across the gulf between species to touch the pectoral fin of a passing great white shark. Initial fears that the legendary predators might smash wildly into cages to try to attack divers proved unfounded. But for exploratory bites and nudges, most great whites behaved cautiously around the antishark cages.

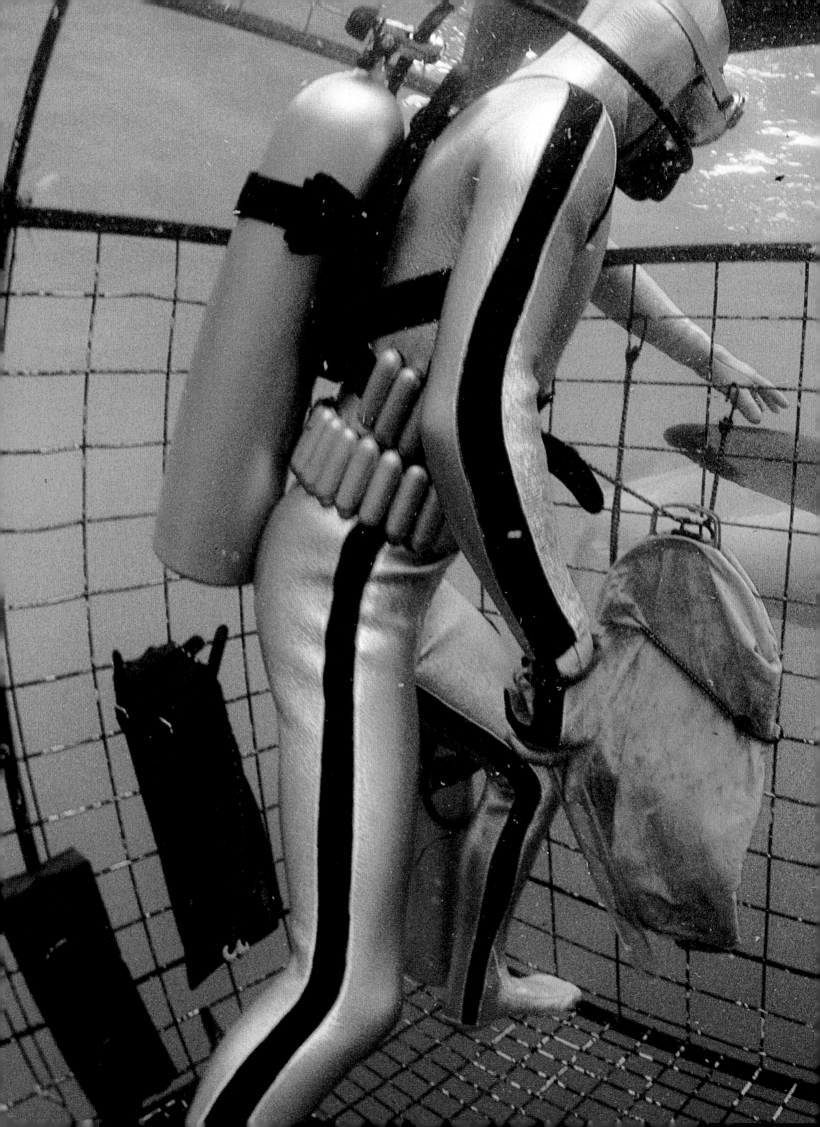

natured visitor, artist Dominique Serafini, to the imposing close-up view of great whites from the cages, an experience that had become routine for the dive team by now. With a quirky, dry wit as formidable as his talent, Dominique is always a welcome guest on expedition. For years now he has been the genius behind a series of cartoonlike Cousteau books published in Paris—of a genre called *bandes dessineés* that is most identified with the Lucky Luke and Tintin books. Dominique, who spends most of his time aboard a ship anchored off Martinique, has turned dozens of Cousteau missions into compelling stories enjoyed in France by readers of all ages.

When we were first envisioning a great white shark expedition, Dominique thought it would make a first-rate

volume in his series, and he asked to spend some time in the field, so that his drawings of the great whites would be as accurate as possible. Since he is a veteran diver, I agreed heartily.

I did not realize that he intended to turn one of our antishark cages into a studio and to spend hours sketching his subjects underwater. But when he arrived on deck in diving gear toting pencils and a plastic pad, I recognized a novel film story in the making and sent Chuck Davis below with his motion picture camera to document our unconventional artist at work. Inspired

Cousteau illustrator Dominique Sérafini sketches the sea's most formidable fish from a viewpoint both illuminating and discomforting. Sharks occasionally tried to bite Sérafini's feet through the cage floor as he worked.

by Dominique's jaunty comportment, the team got into the act. As soon as the cage slipped below the surface, with at least three large sharks nearby, they tossed a bucketload of blood and fish bits into the water, aiming so that the mess billowed down through the liquid sky toward Dominique's head, like a red shower. The water cleared quickly, but the effect was such that one of the sharks became enormously curious about the divers in the cage and began nudging his snout and open mouth against the floor screen beneath Dominique's feet. Dancing as if a gunslinger was shooting at his feet, the artist hopped just ahead of the moving snout, and Davis alertly captured the burlesque on film. (The commentary that accompanied this scene in our television special noted that a dedicated artist will

risk life and limb for his art, and accordingly Serafini would risk his feet.)

With the instincts of an accomplished actor, Dominique watched the shark depart, then turned to the camera and made a deft gesture with his hands to mimic the biting jaws, while nearly popping his eyeballs from their sockets, a bit of Chaplinlike improvisation that made it into the final version of the film.

ABOVE:
Sérafini discusses his sketches with Alcyone's team. The bearded diver is Chuck Davis, who doubled as a film cameraman and still photographer.

OVERLEAF:
Sérafini's rough studies comprised a catalog of expedition life, both above and below the surface.

An accomplished caricaturist as well as illustrator, Sérafini captured the personality of each crew member in drawings he left behind as gifts when he departed.

Later in the *carré*, as I watched him finish a dozen watercolor portraits of the sharks amid the cages, it occurred to me that most readers of the upcoming book would assume that it was painted from photographs by an artist who never left his studio.

Another spate of stormy days not only sent us rushing back to Port Lincoln, but forced us to wonder aloud for the first time if we had reconvened the expedition too hastily in the (apparently erroneous) belief that winter was over in the southern ocean. After three days in port we returned to Dangerous Reef during a lull in the storm, anchored, commenced chumming, greeted a single (tagged) shark, and beat a retreat to Port Lincoln again when conditions worsened after only eight hours. Two days later we managed to endure at Dangerous Reef for twelve hours, returning this time not under an attack of foul weather but because of a shipboard accident that required some medical attention for Antoine Rosset. When a Port Lincoln doctor had finished threading six stitches into his thumb, we headed for Dangerous Reef again.

We lasted there twenty-eight hours under a sky so overcast that there was insufficient light for undersea filming. *Rosy* showed up, along with a tagged eleven-foot male we called *Thierry*, and an eleven-foot female named *Amy*. The day's only moment of interest was provided by *Amy*. After failing several times to snag a bait line being jerked before her, she seemed, in the words of an astonished Paul Martin, to "just fleep out." In apparent frustration, she began chomping furiously with her head raised in the air as she lurched forward across the surface for about fifteen seconds. It brought to mind those chattering wind-up teeth sold in toy stores, although in her case, the relentless biting was in slow motion.

It was not the first time we had seen such a display. During the previous mission, a shark named *Cindy* had behaved in similar fashion. At the time, I recalled, the team thought she might be sick. Two or three crew members began to refer to her as "that dumb shark." But Rocky Strong, who was of course fascinated by the incident, believed that her frustration was so intense it had caused her to "lock on" in response to the most basic aggressive behavior in her repertoire—biting.

The events of the next day, August 26, are best described by quoting from Steve Arrington's journal:

0600: Raised anchor and moved to the south side of Dangerous Reef after the winds shifted from southwest to northeast.
1010: Raised anchor and shifted further south as winds increased.
1130: Raised anchor and sailed for Port Lincoln as the weather continued to worsen.

On August 28, Arrington made another entry:

Because of her mostly flat bottom, Alcyone tends to slam rather heavily into an oncoming sea, causing a shudder that runs the entire length of the ship. For the past two days and nights, the disconcerting shudder has repeated every few seconds as the ship is battered by waves and winds gusting to 30 knots plus. Water sprays the bridge as small waves break over the stern, and continuous rocking makes even the simplest chores difficult. The most incredible aspect of the situation is that Alcyone is taking this beating while we are in a sheltered harbor—tied up to a pier!

Yet it is on occasions like this that one begins to appreciate the vessel's Turbosail system. The shipboard computers are set to automatically orient the ship's tubular sails into the wind, even as it shifts constantly. We can use the same wind which is stirring up the sea to hold the windship safely away from the pier.

Working in the ship's carré, *Sérafini applies final touches to a watercolor depicting expedition* work. The painting will become a panel in a picture book about the mission published in France.

The next day, with the winds decreasing, we returned to Dangerous Reef. According to our schedule, there would be only a few days remaining before the expedition ended, and we had no intention of spending them at a dock. The weather cooperated to a limited extent, providing enough calm for safety but seas too choppy for underwater filming. Capkin, poking about in boredom for something to do, began tinkering with an idea for a measuring line to increase the accuracy of our length estimates. He spaced knots a meter apart along a rope that he tied to the end of a bait line. He reasoned that during the moment or two when a shark was ripping away a bait, the rope would fall along the length of its body. By quickly counting the knots, the deck team could make a fairly accurate estimate of the shark's size. The primitive device fit the

120

requirements of most successful inventions: it was simple. Moreover, it worked. Through the rest of the expedition and those that followed, the accuracy of our length estimates seemed far more reliable than before. We found, as a matter of fact, that tagged sharks we had previously measured by eye often turned out to be a foot or more longer than we had guessed.

In one of the expedition's most dramatic moments, the eleven-foot female named Amy hovered for a full twenty seconds in front of chief diver Arrington in the clear cylinder. Arrington believes that the shark was not poised to attack but seemed to be inspecting. When a dead tuna was substituted for a diver in the cylinder, sharks appeared more interested in finding a way to break into the cage.

A scar and the mangled dorsal fin of the thirteen-foot female called Foxy are thought to be the result of a fight with another great white, or possibly from a mating tangle.

On August 31, we were able at last to send a crew below for filming. Though the dive was unremarkable generally, an incident occurred that produced a marvelous cinematic image, perhaps the best shot of all in the hour-long television special compiled from the expedition. While Deloire's camera was rolling in a nearby steel cage, the eleven-foot female named *Amy* suddenly became inordinately curious about Steve Arrington, who was hanging motionless in the plastic cylinder. She swept leisurely up to the side of the broad tube and froze in place, pectoral fins outstretched like airplane wings, snout fixed to the clear wall, mouth hanging open casually, eyes trained on the diver. She was not attacking; she was inspecting, she was studying. For a full twenty seconds she peered at the bubble-belching stranger in her realm, as if her curiosity had gotten the best of her and she was determined to stare at this puzzle until she figured it out.

For Arrington, of course, the episode was the highlight of the expedition, perhaps of his entire diving career. There was no fear involved, he told us later, since the shark appeared docile. He paused in describing the feeling, then said that it was something like being near a calm tiger at a moment when there was no threat, when the creature was languid. "She was just hovering before me, hugging the cylinder," Steve said, "looking at me as if to say, 'Who are you? What are you?' I can never again think of these sharks as being the crazed killers I once thought."

Six hours later, while Davis and Arrington were below shooting stills on the last dive of the day, the largest shark we were to see during the entire two-year expedition arrived at the stern. Capkin's measuring line indicated that the female (named *Bertha*) was at least eighteen feet long, approaching the size of the largest great white shark ever reliably measured—a nineteen-and-a-half-foot specimen captured in 1987 off Ledge Point in Western Australia. Some great white sharks, while perhaps never reaching the twenty-five feet of "Bruce," the fictional fish of *Jaws* fame, may well exceed twenty feet in length. There have been plenty of unofficial reports of white sharks ranging from twenty to twenty-four feet—even a highly questionable sighting of a twenty-nine-and-a-half footer in the Azores—but our scientific team is extremely careful in dealing with the statistic of size in great whites, perhaps since it seems to inflate not only the public's fascination with the creature but the sensational fear of it.

I suspect one day we will have a well-documented capture of a great white that exceeds twenty feet. Not every report of a supershark has come from self-promoting fishermen or publicity seekers. Ron and Valerie Taylor, whose reputation in such matters is beyond reproach, have sighted individuals alongside their boat which they firmly believe were in the range of twenty-three to twenty-five feet. But until such a huge fish is carefully measured by a researcher and dutifully photographed for posterity, Barry Bruce and Rocky Strong will allow only that the species has for certain reached a length of nineteen-and-a-half feet.

Which, as Robin Milton Love might conclude, is not exactly chicken fat.

During the last three days of this third expedition, we tagged and named two sharks destined to linger for a long time in our memories. They were not terribly unusual. *Mathilda* was a twelve-and-a-half-foot female who hung about *Alcyone*'s stern most of August 30 and 31 before departing. *Foxy*—who showed up on the last day at Dangerous Reef, September 1, and was named in honor of Rodney Fox—was about six inches longer and notable mostly for several recent bite marks along her back

and dorsal fin, possibly gained during a shark fight or a mating tangle. She appeared quite shy, always remaining beyond the other sharks present.

A few months after we had docked *Alcyone* in Port Adelaide and the team had dispersed on holidays or other assignments, Barry Bruce called me at my office in Los Angeles. He sounded uncharacteristically solemn as he told me that our tagging program had produced its first results. Reports had come to his office in the Fisheries Department that three of our tagged great whites had been captured already.

The shy, freshly wounded shark we called *Foxy* had been killed in a commercial fishing net north of Kangaroo Island—a distance of about 130 miles from Dangerous Reef. Her capture had come some seventy-eight days after receiving our tag.

Also snagged in a commercial net was the small shark we had tagged on August 16 and named *Tiny*. Barry was dismayed especially by this capture, because it dashed his hopes that the youngster might mature before being hauled in, giving not only interesting data about his whereabouts later in life, but accurate information about his rate of growth. *Tiny*'s demise had also come near Kangaroo Island, 73 days and 137 miles from his tagging at Dangerous Reef.

Finally, the female known as *Mathilda* had been caught by a game fisherman only about twenty miles east of Port Lincoln. She had been at liberty only thirty days since our tagging, and died only eleven miles from Dangerous Reef. Barry said he would try to reach the fisherman and obtain a photo of the trophy we knew as *Mathilda*.

I recall thinking as I listened to Barry that there would be plenty of time to ponder the behavioral meaning of the captures. Two of the sharks had travelled a good distance, one had not. The taking of three of our tagged sharks in such a short time could only increase our concern over the rate at which the population was being depleted.

But what stuck in my mind had nothing at all to do with science. I realized that nameless great whites would always remain nothing more than a subject for statistics, that they could easily be regarded as perils to human swimmers, better eliminated for the public good. But once an animal had a name, the veil of obscurity disappeared and the potential for remorse was possible—even when the animal was a great white shark. It was no longer simply a fish that took a fishing line; it was an animal with an identity, and the notion of it hanging upside down beside a proud fisherman was somewhat disconcerting. We had seen *Foxy*, *Tiny*, and *Mathilda* up close, had obliquely touched them in the act of tagging and naming them. They were just sharks, but they were now *our* sharks, and, to our genuine surprise, we cared.

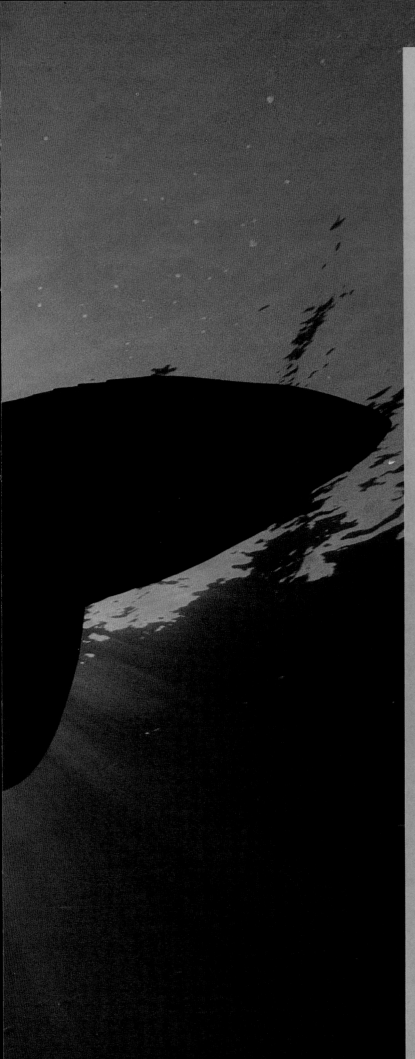

FIVE THE LONELY LORD OF THE SEA

*I should like to think there
will always be a tiger
somewhere in the forest
and a great white shark
somewhere in the sea.*
VALERIE TAYLOR

Hours before we boarded flights to South Australia for our fourth great-white-shark expedition, the Gulf War broke out in Iraq. The media warned of retaliatory terrorist attacks, and airport security was greatly intensified. Airport guards in Los Angeles regarded three of us suspiciously as we checked thirty-eight pieces of luggage containing film and science gear.

A remark at the time by one of the team members revealed how much our attitudes had changed toward the object of our studies. He told us that his wife was relieved that he would not be traveling to Europe during these days of potential terrorist activity, but would be safely away in Australia diving with great white sharks.

Among the sophisticated equipment in our baggage was a device based on a two-thousand-year-old invention called the Archimedes screw. Rocky Strong was intent on standardizing the volume of blood and meat bits entering the water during our chumming operations. His notion was to automate the process in some way, so that a consistent trickle of bait would create a similar odor corridor in each of the sites we visited. Local folklore and the experiences of people like Rodney Fox were the only indicators of where great whites congregated along the South Australia coast. But if the baiting was standardized, and if the sharks tended regularly to arrive more quickly in one place than in another, one could identify those locations where sharks tended to be in close proximity with some supportive data.

Prior to the fourth expedition, Rocky worked with Jim McKibben, a friend in Southern California whose company had supplied pingers for our earlier tracking experiments, to devise a mechanism that would deliver the chum at a precise rate. In a wonderful leap of the imagination, McKibben recalled the machine invented by Archimedes to raise water from the Nile to

Bathed in sunlight and mystery, a great white glides imperially above the lens of photographer Bob Talbot.

Christophe Jouet-Pastre, who served as Alcyone's captain during two white-shark expeditions, ladles an extra helping of chum into waters off the stern. Meanwhile, blood trickles from the team's specially built chum machine, designed to dispense a precisely measured flow of bait.

Rocky Strong makes notes while communicating with the team above through an AquaCom—a mask outfitted with a single-sideband transceiver.

126

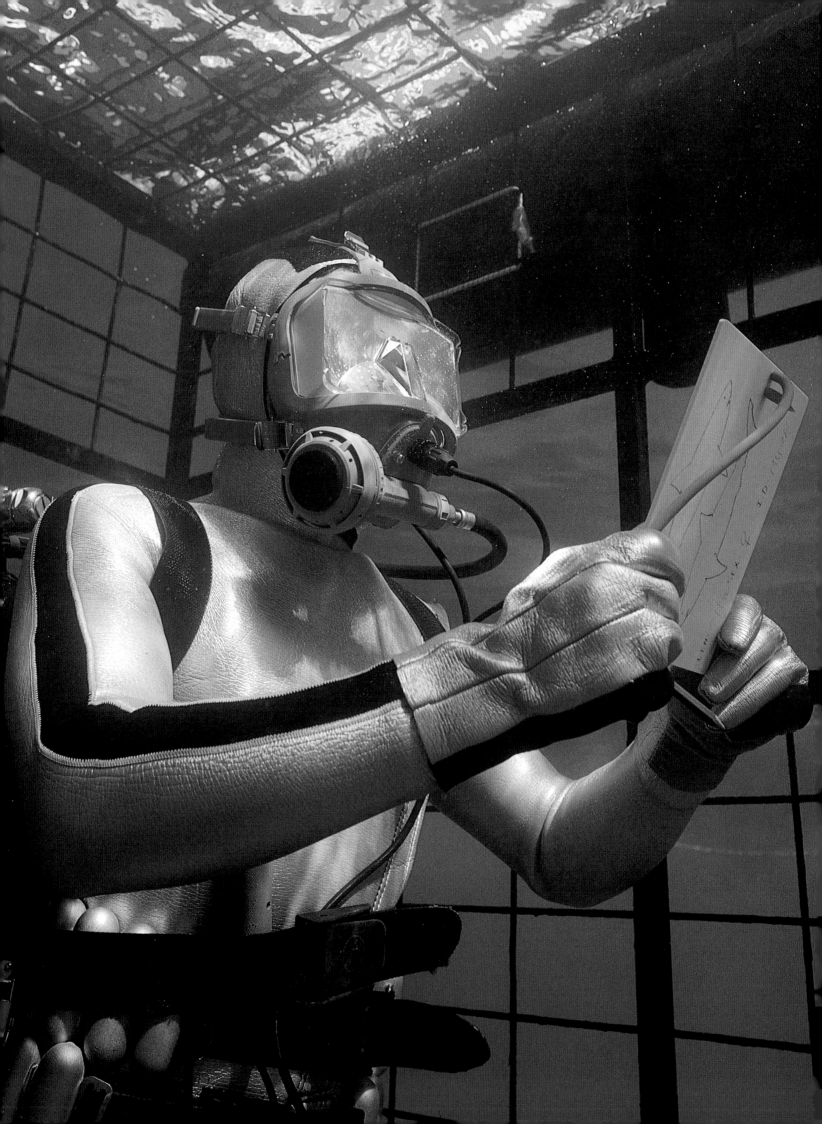

RIGHT:
Gicquel, Arrington, and Richards track Murf *from the* Titanic. *Dangerous Reef is in the background.*

RIGHT INSET:
The Cousteau scientific team checks out the ultrasonic receiver, which enabled the team to monitor both the direction and depth of sharks during trackings. Rocky Strong is at left; Barry Bruce of the South Australian Department of Fisheries is at right, holding the transmitter that will be secured to a shark's back, and the directional hydrophone used to monitor transmitter pings.

BELOW:
Murf, a twelve-foot female tracked on two occasions by the Cousteau team, sports both a fisheries tag and an ultrasonic transmitter (partially wrapped in blue tape). Murf *was a frequent visitor to* Alcyone, *and her tracked routes suggested she might be a resident of the waters surrounding Dangerous Reef.*

ABOVE:
Manipulating bait lines, the team tries to draw Pascale *close enough to be tagged. From left, in the launch dubbed* Titanic: *Strong, Antoine Rosset (with camera), and engineer Patrick Allioux.*

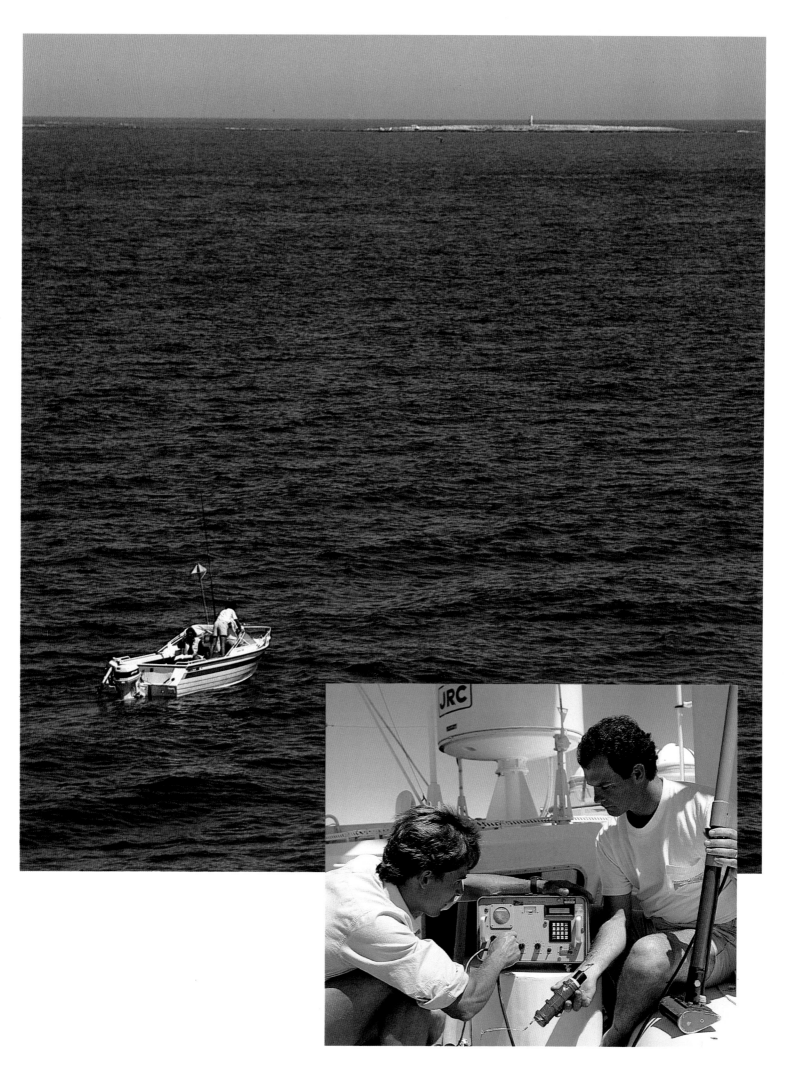

Barry Bruce fills out fisheries tag forms in Alcyone's carré. It was his concern over the possible depletion of South Australia's great white sharks that led Department of Fisheries authorities to initiate a study of the population, which he now directs.

irrigate the fields of ancient Egypt. The principle is simple: a rotating screw within a cylinder carries water upward to a higher level. McKibben fashioned a cylinder that withdrew our liquid chum from a bait bucket and fed it at a consistent rate into the sea. When the gadget was carried onto *Alcyone*'s rear deck, I was amused to see that this machine from humanity's distant past would toil in the shadow of the ship's Comsat satellite dish, which provided us with navigational information from space.

As Rocky was setting up his chum machine, he posed a question that had never occurred to me. If indeed great white sharks were drawn to islands where sea lions or other pinnipeds hauled out, how did the sharks identify these islands from underwater? Did they simply inspect island after island until they encountered diving pinnipeds?

Rocky thought it might be something different. From years of experience, he knew that strong-smelling waste matter and oily secretions wash from pinniped colonies into the sea. He wondered if pinnipeds inadvertently created their own natural odor corridors that attracted passing sharks.

We would not be able to test such a theory, but if our standardized chumming showed a direct correlation between islands bearing pinnipeds and increased shark abundance, such a notion would be worth investigating.

We carried aboard another interesting technological breakthrough that would further the cause of science on this expedition. We had been frustrated throughout the prior missions as we tried to document the dive team's underwater observations of shark behavior. We were limited to their recollections as they emerged from a dive, or the sparse notes scribbled on a plastic notepad kept in the cage. Eventually, it would be possible to study the film they shot as well, but our cameras could not be running during an entire dive.

The solution came in the form of a new communications device which combined an MK-II AGA mask with a single-sideband transceiver, developed by a California company called Ocean Technology Systems, and dubbed AquaCom. The mask contained a wireless radio transmitter, enabling our divers to broadcast their observations back to us on deck continually as events were unfolding undersea. Sound engineer Mike Westgate connected our radio receiver to a tape recorder and a time-code generator, and the result was what Rocky referred to as an "event recorder." The team's close-range observations could be recorded in great detail instantly, and the tape record could be analyzed to measure with some precision such matters as the length of time consumed in certain behavior patterns or the pace of a shark's tail beats. For the first time, we could accumulate numerical data about white-shark behavior, not merely general impressions drawn from memory.

The advances in our scientific program did not extend to weather control, however, and we began this expedition as we had finished the last—buffeted by heavy winds and swells. During our first day at Dangerous Reef, we sighted Anne-Marie, a female tagged during expedition two, and we tagged a new, twelve-foot shark, which was named Murf after Dr. Richard C. Murphy, a dear friend who has directed our scientific and educational programs for some twenty-five years. The rough seas made diving impossible, however, and they continued to hamper our work during the next four days.

Finally, on January 25, the winds abated and, seemingly as a token of our changing fortunes, an impressive great white

arrived at the stern. She was sixteen feet long and broad of girth, the second largest shark we would observe in South Australia. A nylon fishing leader trailed from beneath her, evidence that we were not the first humans to cross her path. In honor of our newest crew member, navigator Pascal Pique, she was christened Pascale.

While organizing this expedition, we had decided to make the tracking of sharks a priority, so, after attaching two fisheries tags to Pascale, we immediately set about trying to implant a sonic pinger as well. Pascale eluded the spear for nearly four hours, but at last Barry managed to pin the transmitter on her right side just below the dorsal fin. The Archimedes screw was unplugged, the anchor weighed, the tracking boat launched, and we set out to shadow through the evening and approaching night a huge gray fish.

The pursuit lasted twenty-six hours. For nearly nine hours, Pascale swam downstream, crisscrossing our odor corridor and generally following a circling pattern. Then she struck out in a northerly direction, traveling from one island to another as she entered Spencer Gulf. This time our spying mission was halted, not by dolphins or any other auditory interference, but by the transmitter itself, which apparently fell from Pascale's side.

Later, as Rocky entered every detail of the episode into Alcyone's computer, and navigator Pique completed a chart of the tracking, I reflected on what would be recorded forever in scientific notations about the last twenty-six hours—quantitative data and a scattering of lines on a map—and on what would not be noted, the human side of tracking a great white shark. The research papers to issue from our work would not characterize the cold, raw night endured by some twelve souls, the biting sea spray kicked into their faces by twenty-knot winds, the hours of conversation among men hunched in darkness in a lonely launch (during which personal histories were shared), or the stomach-turning motions of a boat bobbing about on choppy seas. Scientists would one day read that during our watch Pascale swam a total distance of forty-four miles—losing her transmitter thirteen miles from Dangerous Reef on a direct line. But that is not what chief diver Steve Arrington would recall from the tracking. He would remember enduring one of the worst bouts of seasickness in his life, of spending hour upon hour trying to carry on scientific work with his head hanging over the side of a leaky boat named Titanic.

Three days of chumming passed before another shark arrived. By now, certain great whites—or at least their names—were becoming familiar, and the appearance of these returnees both surprised and pleased the team. On January 29, the shark we called Amy came to the floating baits behind Alcyone. She held

a special place in our memory, since it was *Amy* who, during the last expedition, had hovered with pectorals outstretched as if to hug the plastic cylinder while Arrington returned her stare from inside it.

Since our records indicated that *Amy* had appeared during each of the last three expeditions, and was possibly a resident shark, we decided to bestow upon her a unique honor. She would become our one-and-only computerized great white shark.

Rocky pulled from a case of science gear a small aluminum tube the size of a cigar. Within this nondescript little container there was a lithium-battery-powered microprocessor that controlled a special sensor. At regular intervals, determined by a time chip, the tiny computer awoke and entered into its memory the ambient water depth and temperature. This unit, developed by a Washington-based company called Wildlife Computers, would enable us to document the vertical path of a great white shark over a long period of time. We were most curious to learn if a white shark might venture into deep water off the Continental Shelf, and, proportionately, how much of its time is spent in shallow coastal waters. With the miniature computer, such information could be gathered during months without the need for an immense tracking operation involving boats and people.

There was a serious drawback to the device, however, at least when applied to the animal we were studying. Within three years—the maximum memory-storage life of the unit—the computer had to be retrieved from the great white shark bearing it, so that the memory board within could be interrogated and the data retrieved.

There seemed only two ways to accomplish this. One was to await the possible capture of the subject shark by a fisherman. But Rocky had another scheme in mind, and the entire crew listened in rapt attention as he described it. If, after a month or so, the shark should return to *Alcyone*, we could attempt to anesthetize the animal and regain our little computer from its side.

Incredulous smiles broke out among the assembled team.

Rocky continued. To immobilize such a huge creature, a tremendous volume of tranquilizer would be needed. Rocky had, in fact, brought along the appropriate anesthetic—a chemical compound called MS–222, which is routinely used to immobilize fish and other cold-blooded animals for laboratory

research or transport. The only way Rocky could imagine delivering a sufficient amount of MS–222 into a white shark was to entangle the creature in a net off *Alcyone*'s stern, then reach into its mouth and propel a great burst of the chemical down its throat.

The team wanted to know who would man the squirt gun.

When Rocky quickly explained that he would perform that task, the sighs of relief were heaved in unison. I noticed a glimmer in the eyes of chief cameraman Deloire. While characteristically skeptical, he seemed already to be planning the logistics of filming what would surely be one of the most spectacular scenes in the history of wildlife documentaries.

As it happened, the opportunity to attempt this extraordinary feat never presented itself.

However, at 3:30 P.M. on January 29, as *Amy* made a close pass at a chunk of horsemeat near the stern, Rocky managed to attach the time-depth computer to her. As far as we know, she may still be carrying the device, and if she is hauled in by a fisherman one day, we may be able to produce new and exciting data about the activities of a great white shark across a long period of time.

Two days later, we managed to secure a pinger to the twelve-foot female we called *Murf*, and to initiate our sixth conventional tracking of a great white. Attempts to implant the transmitter had consumed nearly the entire day, and it was 10:30 P.M. before Rocky succeeded, so the pursuit began while most of the crew slept. *Murf* quickly proved content to wander in wide circles about Dangerous Reef, as if she were a security guard patrolling the area through the night.

A curious change had begun to occur in the perceptions of the team as, time and again, they rotated through four-hour shifts aboard the tracking boat. The topic came up now over breakfast, as we discussed the all-night trailing of *Murf*. While they marked the bearings and depth of these sharks, plotting their three-dimensional trajectory in the hunting field of the sea, the men had begun imagining the plight of these great fish. Constantly knowing their whereabouts, following their ceaseless wanderings, they had gained a sense of the loneliness of such an existence. For them, the great white shark had begun to lose its aura of invincibility and its image of viciousness. It now seemed to them merely another animal searching hard for the means to survive a hostile world. Our pencil lines marking a shark's path through only one day, when projected by the imagination across the creature's entire life, suggested a grim and solitary pursuit of food that seemed endless.

The next morning, some twelve hours into the tracking, *Murf* rose to the surface only twenty feet from *Titanic*. For nearly

While surface swimmers glimpse only a terrifying shape in the water and game fishermen see only a hooked and furious opponent, divers behold the more common reality of the great white shark—an immense fish elegant of form and graceful of motion, a silent master of its watery realm.

fifteen minutes she seemed to remain motionless, as if trying to understand a puzzling situation. In the tracking boat, Arrington, Bruno Gicquel, and veteran Cousteau writer Mose Richards were convinced that the shark had turned the tables on them, had risen to take a close look at whomever or whatever had been tailing her through the night. Rocky mentioned another possibility, that the shark was merely "basking." Flight logs of a pilot searching for whales off the California coast some forty years ago include more than one hundred sightings of great white sharks moving slowly along the sea surface.

The surveillance of *Murf* lasted nearly twenty-eight hours, the longest tracking we would achieve. It could have gone on longer, but Rocky elected to call it off because there was no indication that *Murf* intended to do anything but continue to patrol the waters off Dangerous Reef. Though the tracking boat had covered a distance of forty-seven miles during the pursuit, *Murf* never roamed more than a few miles from the island, and was only four miles from Dangerous Reef when we ended the operation.

Two nights later, when *Murf* reappeared at our baits, we decided to verify our conclusions about her movements. Since the pinger on her back was still broadcasting, we set out behind her once more in the tracking boat for nearly twelve hours. Again, while covering a total distance of sixteen miles, she remained in the vicinity of the reef and was only two miles from it when we called the tracking off at 10:00 A.M.

We anchored *Alcyone* near Dangerous Reef again, and activated the Archimedes screw to reestablish the odor corridor that had dissipated during the all-night tracking. Since the seas were flat, we organized a dive using both steel cages, and since the chumming had only recently begun again, we felt safe in stepping out of the cages to explore the bottom for a short time. I had in mind to reenact for the camera a scene that had taken place during a previous dive. While standing unprotected on the bottom, camera poised to shoot a shark passing overhead, Deloire had suddenly begun to jump about like a man possessed. The rest of the dive team was concerned, until they realized that Michel had blundered into an assemblage of crabs, which were pinching his feet. The moment had gone unrecorded on film, and I wanted to see if it could be recreated.

Capkin, Deloire, and I stepped out of one cage to look about for crabs, while Arrington and visiting diver David Brown ventured forth from the other. We were outfitted not for swimming but for standing in the cages—wearing no fins and burdened with a second weight belt to maintain stability while standing erect. The setting was interesting, and we strolled about like overweight hikers in a meadow.

On the deck, however, there was a moment of high consternation. Through the radio receiver, Arrington could be heard shouting suddenly into the AquaCom mask: "Shark present! Shark present! Get in the cage, in the cage! The shark's coming in at six o'clock! Whup, here she comes now about eighteen feet off the bottom!"

Unable to do anything but listen, the crew gathered about the radio to hear a play-by-play description of a potential catastrophe taking place below.

Only a minute after reaching the bottom, when all five of us had wandered some ten to fifteen yards from the safety of the cages, Arrington had caught sight of *Murf* emerging from the shadow cast down through the water column by *Alcyone*. The shark was gliding toward the dive team. Slowed by water density and the extra weight belt, Arrington immediately began trudging about the bottom to grab the arm of each diver and point at the approaching great white.

As I realized the nature of what was transpiring, I was struck not only by the potential terror of the situation, but by its absurdity. Fear and engrossment seemed to mingle in my mind as I watched my friends attempting to rush back to their steel shields, turned by the conditions and their equipment into slow-motion runners whose every step kicked up a delicate cloud of sand. Deloire, stubbornly adamant about filming without bars before him, seemed to misunderstand the reason Arrington grabbed his shoulder and was about to go on about his business. Frustrated, Arrington used his hands to mime the clashing of jaws, and Deloire grudgingly turned toward the nearest cage.

Just as the last of us had scooted to safety, *Murf* slid past, eyes flicking slightly to assess the situation. Perhaps she would have attacked one of us had we not reached the cages. But all my instincts told me at the time that she would not have been aggressive, that she would have merely glided past curiously, at least once. I guess Deloire felt the same way. As soon as the shark was fifty feet beyond his cage, he stepped back out, camera whirring.

The next two weeks proved to be a test of our resolve. Storm front followed storm front. Diving was out of the question most days. Spirits sagged as the tedium of waiting stretched on and on. The Archimedes screw churned out chum, and the bait lines were launched and relaunched, and the team took turns searching the waters for the dun-colored spot that signaled an approaching shark, and nothing happened at all. Well, *Murf* did make an occasional appearance, snapping at a bait or two and then departing before a camera could be dispatched to the stern. And not another member of her species came near enough to be sighted.

Jean-Michel welcomes Australian diver and photographer Valerie Taylor aboard Alcyone. Taylor, one of the world's most famous divers and a longtime observer of white shark behavior, joined the Cousteau team not only to dive with sharks but to share knowledge of the great white gained during countless expeditions.

We decided to try another site, and sailed to South Neptune Island. There, on February 16, we tagged two males, a fifteen-footer (*Jacques*) and one that reached nearly eleven feet (*Jule*). Of these, the smaller great white was the more interesting. *Jule* carried tattered remnants of a fishing net that appeared tightly wrapped about each pectoral fin. There was a good deal of scarring along one of his sides, too. But what most intrigued us was *Jule*'s odd swimming stroke. He actually appeared ungainly and erratic as he swung his tail to and fro, sometimes beating the water inefficiently with the tail half exposed above the water's surface. When he changed direction abruptly, his head would swing around, while his pectoral fins and tail dropped awkwardly. We managed to videotape one of his ascents, as he headed rocketlike for the surface at a 90-degree angle. I found Rocky's lighthearted descriptions of this strange shark to be both refreshingly unscientific and amusing. "This guy goes ballistic," Rocky said.

Jule was definitely an exception rather than the rule. While some observers, after only limited time with great whites, have described them as typically ungainly, we found their maneuvering impressive generally. There were sometimes marked differences between individuals, and some appeared unsure as a result of confusion in our artificial feeding conditions, but most of the sharks seemed neither erratic nor inept as predators.

Of greater scientific interest, perhaps, was the gender of these two sharks—two males in water that was several degrees colder than that surrounding Dangerous Reef, where we had so far sighted twenty-two females and only four males. (The gender of seven sharks at Dangerous Reef had gone undetected.) Our theory that females tended to seek out warmer water than males—perhaps because such conditions favor the survival of their young at birth—seemed to gather support.

On February 17, we returned to Port Lincoln and welcomed aboard *Alcyone* two celebrities of the diving world—American photographer Bob Talbot and Australian Valerie Taylor. Though he has joined us on many Cousteau expeditions as an underwater cameraman and photographer, Bob is best known to the general public for his extraordinary photographic studies of dolphins and whales. Posters with his characteristic signature evoke the magic and grace of these creatures in a singular style popular among art collectors as well as nature lovers.

Valerie Taylor and her husband Ron are among the best-known divers in the world, and their pioneering film work has won accolades for more than thirty years. Millions of television viewers remember a film shot by Ron in which Valerie, outfitted

Two veterans of shark diving descend as a team—Deloire to film while Valerie Taylor, right, acts as a lookout and still photographer.

in a steel-mesh suit, practically forces her arm into the mouth of a blue shark. They were part of the film teams that shot both *Blue Water, White Death* and the live-action scenes for *Jaws*. They have probably captured more film of sharks than any other filmmakers, and have spent as much time observing them as any other shark specialists.

Their stories, and their good fellowship, have filled many evenings in my life, and it was as a close friend that I prevailed upon Valerie to come aboard *Alcyone* and dive with our team. Ron and Valerie are unpretentious people and I could see discomfort in Valerie's eyes when our young diving crew treated her with the deference accorded a superstar. When I began to draw white-shark stories from her over a welcoming lunch, the table grew quiet and her words met with the rapt attention of the entire crew.

Valerie, like her friend Rodney Fox, is convinced that there are not as many great whites off the South Australia coast as there were twenty years ago. "They're not as easily attracted," she told us, "they're not as aggressive, and they're not of the size we used to see. It's as if they're frightened, as if they've learned that man and his boats are dangerous."

One of the younger team members asked the inevitable question: what was her most dangerous moment with a white shark? Valerie answered by telling us several astonishing stories, and she did so in such a gentle, unassuming manner that she might have been recounting trips to the supermarket. One story in particular amazed us.

"In 1972," she recalled, "Ron and I were suspended in a steel cage filming a twelve-foot male great white. Suddenly the shark rose to the surface and, with its snout, bumped the steel trace line from which the cage was hanging. Startled for some reason, the shark flicked backwards, twisting the steel line about its head. Now alarmed, it dove and spun about, binding the cable even more firmly about its body.

"The cage plunged and bucked, throwing Ron and me about violently. In panic, the boat crew released the cable, leaving us to be towed on a roller-coaster ride behind the thrashing shark. The air gauge of my Scuba tank became entangled in the cage floor, pinning me down, but Ron was in deeper trouble. He was snorkeling and could breathe only when the cage occasionally emerged from the water for a moment. Sometimes, the cage was underwater for a minute or more.

"It was a wild ride, and we both realized that we could soon be dead. But the shark's wild gyrations, twisting backwards to bite at the wire restraining it, eventually exhausted the creature. It looked to be suffocating. Rodney Fox arrived in a launch and we managed to tow the shark to the shallows along Dangerous Reef. Ron climbed out of the cage and, as calmly as

if he were dealing with a household pet, began unwinding the cable from the shark's body. That done, he pointed its mouth into the current, to help it breathe. I lifted the tail from the water so the creature wouldn't further damage itself by whipping about against the rocks. Amazingly, there were sea lions gathered all around watching this operation. And all the while, the shark kept his eye on Ron. Since the shark lay motionless, Ron gave it a push, and it swam out into deeper water, but then it returned to where Ron stood. He pushed it again, and the great white vanished in a flurry of spray."

The table was silent as Valerie finished this story. She paused, shook her head, and continued. "You see, all these experiences with great white sharks over the years have convinced me of one thing. They are neither friends nor enemies to human beings.

"The very next night after our wild ride in the cage, Ron slipped on the oily boat deck and fell into the water amid three large white sharks. It took him thirty seconds to swim to the boat—which was being carried away by a strong wind and current—and then to reach the rear deck, where he could climb aboard. During that agonizing period, none of the sharks made a move to attack him, and one was watching from directly beneath him when at last he was pulled into the boat. Ron had spared a shark the day before, and that night the sharks returned the favor."

Since our luck had been running better at South Neptune Island, we returned there on the evening of the 17th, established an odor corridor, and welcomed a new, eleven-foot male named *Skura* the next morning. While routinely tossing tuna-bait lines in his direction, we witnessed something that further eroded the imperious reputation of great whites in our eyes. An adult sea lion suddenly appeared alongside the new shark and proceeded to perform swift rolls about it. The shark cruised ahead, seemingly unable to move with sufficient agility to attack or pursue the brazen sea lion. Chuck Davis had told me of observing the same kind of confrontation during an earlier expedition.

Rocky and Valerie agreed that sea lions are known to flaunt their suppleness and speed in the face of their greatest enemy. It may be something like a blue jay and a cat. Often, a wily jay will perch on a branch just beyond the reach of a housecat, and continually hop to a higher branch when the cat lunges and climbs in pursuit. The bird could fly away and forget the cat, but it acts as if it takes great pleasure in tormenting its enemy.

Valerie told of witnessing a shark–sea lion encounter years earlier while filming from a cage underwater. She and a cameraman were watching several white sharks circle their bait

White sharks seem to keep a wary eye out for other members of their species. It appeared to the Cousteau team that the shark closer to the camera was turning its head, possibly to avoid the camera, but more likely to check up on the larger shark behind it. Divers often noticed such behavior.

when an immense white appeared. It may have been eighteen to twenty feet long, and it immediately began to dominate the smaller sharks. The dive site was near a sea-lion colony, and while the two divers watched, a small sea lion zoomed down from the surface and began to spin in circles around the huge shark, rocketing and twisting about in an almost impish display of underwater gymnastics. The white lumbered ahead stiffly.

Gradually, Valerie told us, the shark appeared to grow angry at the agile pinniped.

Then, an extraordinary thing happened. The little sea lion, perhaps carried away in its maneuvers, suddenly found itself suspended for an instant directly in front of the shark's snout. Perhaps realizing that it was a bite away from doom, the sea lion whipped about and dashed to safety behind the diver's

cage, escaping by inches the firing up of violent carnivorous machinery. Valerie's companion was so dumbfounded he forgot to raise his camera for a picture.

It was as if, triggered by the brief glimpse of the offending sea lion in its attack range, perhaps frustrated to a flash point, the large white lost control of its body to the galvanic furies embedded in its muscles by the craftwork of evolution. Its great

This Bob Talbot photograph conveys what a diver sees from the cage just before descending amid great white sharks. When sharks were present, Alcyone's rear deck was crowded with activity.

A plastic decoy duck is about to disappear into the huge maw of a great white shark. To test the shark's selectivity in attacking prey, the team offered a variety of non-food objects. In all cases, including the decoy pictured here, the sharks initially bit the objects in an investigatory fashion, but promptly spit them out. The team concluded that whites are relatively indiscriminate in their test bites, but highly selective in what they swallow.

mouth began chomping and its quivering body lunged toward the sea lion that was no longer there.

Just at that instant, one of the smaller great whites happened to turn a corner and blunder into the same water space occupied a moment earlier by the tiny sea lion. It seemed to recognize its error immediately and to set about halting its glide with every means at its disposal, but it was too late. As the huge white barreled forward, its wildly clapping jaws tore into the side of the arriving shark.

To Valerie, it did not appear that the larger shark intended to bite the smaller, but rather, that once the ancient attack pattern had begun, there was no way of stopping it. In an instant, a mat of flesh the size of a cupboard door was hanging amidships from the smaller shark, and its viscera slipped out as the wounded victim fled.

The giant appeared uninterested in the trail of organs and blood and swam forward leadenly without pursuit. It seemed a simple accident, a misfiring. Gradually, the bellowlike action of the great jaws slowed and the creature resumed its methodical circling of the boat and the stunned divers and the cascade of bait pouring from above.

For two days, heavy swells again prevented us from descending in the cages, even though several sharks were working our bait lines. We used the time, however, to carry out some unscientific experiments regarding the belief that sharks will devour almost anything. There is evidence that white sharks are not as indiscriminate in their feeding as many other shark species, despite the sensational stories that often appear in the popular media.

After concluding with our scientists that biodegradable cardboard was unlikely to harm a great white, Paul Martin tossed an empty cardboard box in the path of a circling shark. The creature passed the object several times before making a slow, direct approach. It bit the box, pulling it underwater in a twisting motion. But within a second or two—as later confirmed during a screening of film capturing the moment—the shark spit the box out and swam away in apparent disinterest.

On occasion team members had seen white sharks attempt to catch cormorants or gulls sitting on the water near *Alcyone*. Once or twice, the attacks had been successful. To the amusement of the crew, I had brought along four plastic duck decoys, and we followed the same procedure, tossing them out on tethers one or two at a time into the blood-saturated water at the stern. Several times a shark rose quickly to engulf a decoy, and in each case, as we expected, the attacker disgorged the fake bird without swallowing it. We could only conclude that the foreign objects seemed unrewarding to the palate of the

great white shark, and that its reputation as an unselective eater was highly questionable.

Throughout this expedition, Rocky had been carrying out a series of critically designed experiments that suggested great whites are also discriminating in what they choose to attack, even in our chum-clouded observation area, if given a choice of prey. Rocky had built a floating device which presented the sharks with two plywood shapes along the surface—one a square and the other a sea-lion silhouette. Based on the responses of seven or eight different white sharks, he had observed a general tendency for the creatures to approach the familiar shape of their sea-lion prey before investigating the novel shape of the square. The point, Rocky believed, was that white sharks may be more dependent on their vision when hunting than has been previously assumed. Despite the stimulus of abundant blood in the water, the creatures seemed not to attack randomly but to make their first attacks on the sea-lion shape, and to commit to these attacks at impressive distances.

Early on the morning of February 21, a new, ten-foot shark appeared at the stern. It was another male, soon christened *Mose*, and it turned out to be the first in a wave of great whites descending on our chum cloud. By 9:00 A.M., there were six, possibly eight, sharks circling *Alcyone*, all of them males. We hurriedly prepared a cage dive, in hopes that Deloire could film scenes of the shark assemblage. Valerie volunteered to accompany Michel as his safety diver, and the two were quickly lowered.

The two veterans opened the top hatch and clambered up to stand unprotected on the roof of the cage, having previously agreed to warn one another of an approaching shark with a jab to the ribs, so they could quickly leap back into the cage. Within moments, while Deloire was turned away to film a shark to starboard, Valerie saw a fourteen-footer suddenly angle down toward them from the port side. She jabbed at Deloire and missed. Before she could make a second attempt to alert him, the shark was upon her. It did not seem to be attacking but rather nudging at her curiously and insistently. Valerie pushed her underwater still camera against the shark's throat, with no noticeable effect, and the momentum of the huge creature began to drive her down through the cage hatch.

Though unaware of what was transpiring behind him, Deloire had a sudden, inexplicable feeling that he should turn around. He confronted an unforgettable scene: within arms reach, Valerie was sliding downward like a tack beneath a giant thumb. Michel whipped his cine camera around as quickly as water density would allow, struck the creature lightly on the snout, and redirected it upwards. The shark left without

Biologist Strong prepares an experiment he designed to test whether great whites would exhibit a preference for objects shaped like natural prey over less familiar shapes. Plywood targets in the shape of a seal and square were floated near each other along the surface.

Despite the possibly confusing stimulus of abundant blood in the water, sharks almost always approached the seal shape first, sometimes biting or rubbing against it. Strong believes that this may indicate that vision is more important as a hunting tool than was previously thought.

inflicting any damage, and the incident turned from potential tragedy to a source of humor for the lunch conversation that followed the dive.

The next day, while restricted to surface filming by mountainous swells, we again came perilously close to losing a team member. Two twelve-to-fourteen-foot sharks were at the stern, and since both were first-time visitors, we were attempting to tag them. Four of the crew were crowded together on the swimstep, each busily attending to their individual tasks. Among them was Bob Talbot, who was leaning from the edge of the platform to photograph the sharks as they passed close to the stern.

As one of the great whites approached, a swell suddenly

lifted the stern, jostling those standing on the swimstep. Talbot, head down and eyes glued to the viewfinder, was bumped accidentally, and he fell forward directly onto the back of the passing white shark. Those nearby froze in horror for a microsecond, then scrambled to grab him.

Bob, meanwhile, found himself glancing off the back of a great white shark, midway between the dorsal and the tail. He felt a swipe of the tail hit his head and realized that his glasses had fallen off. Instinctively, in the confusion of the moment, he grabbed about in the swirling water to find the glasses. It soon occurred to him that retrieving his glasses was not the highest priority under these circumstances, and that he should perhaps think about getting out of the water.

When he surfaced, however, he found himself under the

stern, which was plunging down upon him. He held up his hands to fend off the hull, then managed to bob up into the hands of his eager shipmates, who pulled him aboard. The passing shark did not seem to pose an immediate threat since it simply glided on undisturbed by the crash of a human onto its back, but the whereabouts of the second shark was unknown and the team feared it could attack from below before Bob was hauled in.

Talbot emerged with only one shoe, no glasses, and his prized Nikon F–4 camera saturated with saltwater. The monumental danger of the experience had not yet struck him. He glumly set about trying to cleanse the seawater from his camera and soon realized that his $3,000 instrument was a total loss.

A few minutes after the accident, Mose Richards asked Talbot what emotions he was feeling. "You've just experienced what most people would consider the ultimate nightmare," Mose observed.

"Oh, it could have been worse," Bob declared. "Five minutes before the accident I had my 300mm lens on the camera. I could have lost that, too!"

Mose shook his head in disbelief. "Photographers are different from the rest of us," he said.

But an hour later, when Bob had changed into dry clothes and rejoined us at the stern, I stood beside him as a fourteen-foot white ripped apart a slab of horse meat.

He stared quietly for a moment, then said in hushed amazement: "Could have been me."

The incident provided fodder for shipboard conversations during the rest of the expedition. Initially, we talked about the spectacular nature of what had nearly befallen our friend and shared our relief that Bob had come away unscathed. But as time wore on, we realized that the episode was not only about Bob Talbot, but about the great white shark as well. Before our expeditions had begun, we might have anticipated that a white shark struck in the back by a crashing human would have turned about in fury and bitten the offender. But after months of experience in their midst, after hearing of Ron Taylor's similar mishap among whites, after watching them behave with seeming disinterest or caution around our divers, none of us was surprised that Talbot's shark—its glide rudely interrupted by a tumbling man—merely cruised ahead as if nothing had happened.

On the other hand, as one wag aboard ship suggested, maybe they simply have no appetite for photographers.

The next day, Rocky, Valerie, Mike Westgate, Mose, and I took leave of Alcyone to spend three days attending an international scientific conference on sharks organized by the

Despite sophisticated sensory systems and powerful jaws, adult great whites lack the agility to pursue acrobatic prey like sea lions. The Cousteau team saw sea lions swimming boldly near their immense enemies. The team's observations strongly supported theories that great whites generally resort to sneak attacks to capture such quarry, zooming up from the depths to surprise pinnipeds from behind.

Taronga Zoo in Sydney. En route, as we made our way from Port Lincoln to Adelaide to Sydney, I noticed with increasing concern the number of white-shark jaws for sale in souvenir shops. It is impossible to know how many great whites fall victim to game or commercial fishermen each year, since many sport captures probably go unreported and many incidental catches in commercial nets are tossed back into the sea as worthless dead meat. Yet the scores of cleaned and polished jaws gave me pause. If they represented known captures, how many could be disappearing without our knowledge?

Valerie shared my concern and suggested that while in Sydney I speak with sport-fishing writer Peter Goadby, a long-time acquaintance of hers who is perhaps the best known of Australia's big-game fishermen.

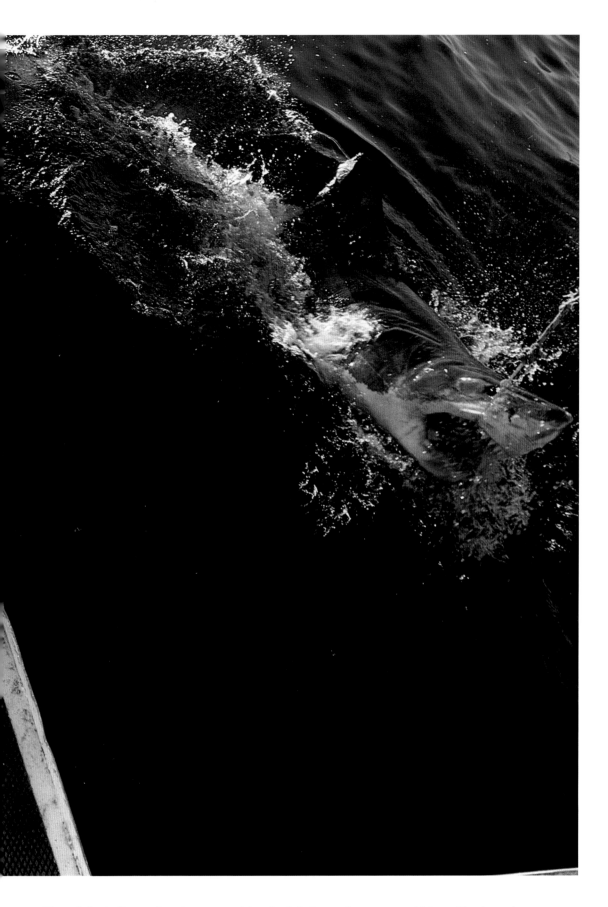

Though he believes that the great white shark is in no danger along most of the Australian coast, Peter is quick to agree that the white shark population in South Australia seems greatly diminished from the past.

"There are fewer since the movie *Jaws* appeared," he said, "because so many have been taken by commercial fishermen who sell the teeth. That's why game fishing for white sharks in

Veteran Cousteau cinematographer Michel Deloire often spent hours waiting for the moment when a great white suddenly emerged to attack a bait.

South Australia is down from perhaps ten catches a year to none or one or two."

Peter explained that some tuna fisherman take advantage of the fact that their catches often attract great whites. While pulling in tuna they also fish for whites off the back of the boat, then sell the jaws.

"The commercial fisherman has got to make a living," Peter said, "and if he can get $3,000 for a set of white-shark jaws or $3,000 for a ton of tuna, its the same to him."

When I asked about the attraction of catching a great white for sport, despite the fact that the species is not a food fish, Peter compared the challenge to that of the mountain climber who dreams of conquering Everest.

"Some of the things done in the past were cruel," he said, "but there's a more humane attitude today, an awareness of the need to conserve the food chain and to protect the peak predators." Peter believes that the trend toward tag-and-release catches among game fishermen bodes well for the future of such desirable species as the great white.

"Hey," he said, "who wants to be the one to catch the last marlin or the last great white shark?"

The scientific conference in Sydney was a similar measure of how far humanity has come in appreciating creatures once deemed enemies. It seemed to us that nearly every shark specialist in the world had come to the Taronga Zoo—from Russia, Trinidad, Japan, the United States, Spain, South Africa, and Mexico, as well as Australia and New Zealand. They were gathered to spend the better part of a week not only comparing notes on their latest findings, but sharing their plans for protecting sharks from human abuse.

During the first afternoon of the conference, Valerie, Ron, and I were asked to judge a delightful contest. In anticipation of this prestigious gathering of shark scientists, many of Sydney's public elementary schools had conducted special classes in shark biology and ecology. Breaking with tradition, teachers emphasized the vital role played by sharks and stressed their diminishing numbers rather than their fearsome weaponry.

Scores of youngsters had come to the zoo that afternoon wearing costumes that depicted their favorite shark species, and we had the high honor of picking the best costumes and bestowing awards upon the excited young winners. When the contest was over, I roamed through exhibits created by the schoolchildren. Dozens of posters caught my eye, each depicting sharks being harmed by humans. "Save the Sharks!" read one poster. "Sharks are not monsters!" declared another. If children can understand this, I thought, even the great white shark may have a future.

I returned to *Alcyone* in high spirits and we sailed back to South Neptune Island, where the team had experienced great luck during my absence. At times, they were filming six or eight whites at the stern. The weather had grown so turbulent, however, that we spent the last two days of the expedition looking for shelter rather than sharks.

We gave up, put in to Port Lincoln, shook hands all around in camaraderie, opened a bottle of champagne to toast the impending marriage of our French engineer Patrick Allioux to a charming girl from Perth, and dispersed in various directions around the world.

I departed in a hopeful mood, certain that events and public awareness were marshalling in favor of the great white shark, increasing the odds that it would one day be better understood and even protected. But months later I was shocked to hear a story passed our way by Port Lincoln fishermen. The claim was that a greedy fisherman or two, perhaps keeping track of our whereabouts by monitoring the marine radio, had sped to the site of our abandoned odor corridors and attempted to harvest in our wake some of the great whites we had attracted.

We could not corroborate the story, but it came from reliable sources. If true, it seemed likely that some of our tagging efforts had been in vain, since unprincipled fishermen surely would not report the details of their illicit captures nor return the spaghetti tags to an agency of the government. If the story was true, we wondered which of our sharks, conditioned briefly in our presence to expect no danger at the stern of a boat, may have fallen victim to the dark side of human nature, may have been attacked mercilessly by men intoxicated with greed— which can render members of our own species more monstrous than any shark in the sea.

Bob Talbot captures an image reflecting both the beauty and haunting drama of the team's undersea work. Beneath a cloud of blood and the ghostly shadow of a crewman on deck holding a plastic billyclub (the only weapon carried by Cousteau divers during the expedition) chief diver Arrington, also with a billyclub, awaits the arrival of a great white shark.

SIX ON BEHALF OF THE GREAT WHITE SHARK

Fear is the main source of superstition, and one of the main sources of cruelty. To conquer fear is the beginning of wisdom.
BERTRAND RUSSELL
An Outline of Intellectual Rubbish

By the time Expedition Four was completed, we had accumulated about 115 hours of film about great white sharks in our Los Angeles editing rooms, and some 10,000 still photographs in our New York photo library. We had set out for Australia two years earlier with the modest goal of filming great whites during a single voyage lasting only about two weeks. Now we had one of the world's largest film and still-photo archives documenting this little-known creature. During the next six months we would produce a one-hour television special, "The Great White Shark: Lonely Lord of the Sea"—chronicling the expeditions in a highly condensed way, and presenting the white shark in a more sympathetic light than perhaps any other film on the subject.

While coproducer and editor David Saxon and assistant editor Steve DeNicola were cutting the film, an opportunity arose for yet another short expedition to Dangerous Reef. Since *Alcyone* was now at work elsewhere, the South Australian Fisheries Department made available its 99-foot research vessel *Ngerin*—Aboriginal for "Good Fishing"—and assigned a crew of ten scientists and sailors led by Rocky Strong and Barry Bruce. Ian Gordon of Sydney's Manley Aquarium also joined the team, providing his expertise in the capture and handling of sharks—in the event that *Amy*, the shark bearing a computer, might return.

This fifth shark mission offered another chance to tag white sharks and to keep an eye out for those we had already tagged. Also, Rocky and Barry were able to organize the diving work to make greater use of the AquaCom mask and event recorder, gathering more detailed quantitative data than ever before

This wall of posters created by school children was exhibited at Sydney's Taronga Zoo during a 1991 international conference of shark scientists called "Sharks Down Under."

The wall of haze below Alcyone's double rear hull and twin stabilizer fins gives the impression of a deep-water setting. In fact, the white shark expedition was carried out in depths ranging from fifty to seventy-five feet.

A seemingly curious great white passes close to the plastic cylinder while Deloire films. At times, sharks pushed their snouts against the plastic walls, producing a sound compared by divers to that of a squeegee against glass.

about interactions among the sharks when more than one was present.

The team set out early in the southern spring and observed great whites for about two weeks, concentrating most of their time at Dangerous Reef. They managed to tag another nine sharks and to identify two individuals tagged during previous visits: *Eva*, who had first appeared a year earlier during

Expedition Three, and the inveterate *Rosy*, who established herself as the shark who had visited us most frequently and over the longest time-span.

Rocky later told me that he came away from this last trip more convinced than ever that great whites are principally daylight feeders. The *Ngerin* team was able to keep precise records of every bait taken during the trip, documenting not only the time each was consumed and the shark involved, but the weight of the meat. Thus, they knew when and how much each shark had ingested. Even when present during the night, the sharks rarely attacked the bait lines until dawn, when wave after wave of bait runs would begin. This seemed further evidence to Rocky that, once sharks are in attack range, vision is perhaps the most important sense for hunting success.

He recalled as well some unexpected observations. One afternoon he watched tommy roughs scraping themselves against *Eva*'s sides as the twelve-foot shark circled at the stern, perhaps cleaning away irritating parasites using the shark's raspy skin. Fish called Rainbow Runners have been observed performing the same kind of hygienic behavior by rubbing against reef sharks.

We had noticed earlier that great whites themselves often carried parasitic isopods and copepods on their skin. Of most interest to Rocky was the apparent mobility of the parasites, which changed positions on the sharks' bodies from one day to the next. At times they would disappear for a day, leading Rocky to believe that the parasites actually entered the cloaca,

gills, or mouth to feed on soft tissue, and perhaps to seek refuge. We think of sharks feeding upon other creatures, but seldom imagine that they are vulnerable to being eaten ever so slowly themselves.

Rocky laughed when he described one incident. It was early in the morning and he was keeping track of a great white that had swept past the baits several times. It happened that the crew had tied an inflatable launch to the port stern quarter of the vessel. As the hungry shark passed by on one sortie it missed the floating bait, swam a few yards farther, and bit powerfully into the little launch, which deflated quickly with a loud whoosh. The rumpled boat was pulled aboard with the crane and inspected. The shark had not swallowed any rubber,

but its bite had inflicted a series of distinct punctures reminiscent of the scars on Rodney Fox's torso. Ironically, the team had planned to use the craft within an hour to visit Dangerous Reef. Hearing this, I felt relieved that we had decided not to employ *Alcyone*'s inflatable Zodiacs during the previous white shark expeditions.

Rocky also told of watching a sea-lion pup arrive at the stern late one night. The youngster was less than a meter in length, and it sculled about slowly, passing back and forth near the floating baits. Rocky said the pup looked pathetically like a sitting duck as it paddled lazily, seemingly unaware that it was lolling about in a realm of great danger. Rocky felt a pang of regret, since the artificial feeding situation at the stern of the boat might be luring a young pinniped to its death.

An hour later Rocky noticed the unmistakable silhouette of a great white swimming deep below the little sea lion. Suddenly, the pup ducked his head below the surface, seeming to spot the shark, and froze for a moment. For several hours afterward the sea lion lingered near the stern of the boat, as if afraid to venture away from the dubious shelter it might offer. Rocky left

A blue shark photographed by Rocky Strong off Southern California is accompanied by jack mackerels, which apparently rub against the shark's rasplike skin to scrape away bothersome parasites. The Cousteau team in Australia witnessed similar behavior by tommy roughs, which darted against the skin of a twelve-foot great white shark as it circled Alcyone.

Since this great white is a male,
its distended belly may be
evidence of a recent substantial
meal, perhaps a sea lion.

the swimstep in case the pup was intelligent enough to realize that the low platform offered a safe perch and suddenly had to leap for its life.

Later, when Rocky was pulling in a current meter, he felt a strong tug on the line. "The little pupper was playing with the meter," Rocky laughed. "To get him to leave this deadly place I picked up some seashells from the deck and threw them at him. He just nosed them playfully as they drifted down in the water."

At times, Rocky could make out the shape of the great white near the pup. "They must have known of each other's presence," Rocky said, "but nothing happened." Finally, about 7:00 A.M., the pup sped off toward shore and never showed up again. Rocky wondered if, under the same conditions during the daytime, the pup might have been attacked, no matter how close to the boat. Was the shark already satiated with food, or incapable of targeting the pup in the darkness, or did it somehow lack the motivation? Rocky didn't have the answer, but he was relieved at the outcome.

Near the end of this abbreviated mission, the team landed at a cove on North Neptune Island and spent several hours surveying a herd of New Zealand fur seals that haul out along the shore. The scientists were curious to know what percentage of the pinnipeds might carry scars that could be associated with great white attacks. Of about 100 fur seals, they could find only three bearing dramatic scars. Two of these scars were roughly crescent-shaped, suggesting a white shark bite, and appeared along the fur seals' rumps—consistent with an attack from behind and below by a great white shark. One small fur seal bore longitudinal scars over most of its body, which may have resulted from entanglement in a net rather than an engagement with a great white.

The team made a similar survey at Dangerous Reef among about seventy sea lions, finding only one bearing the infamous crescent-shaped scar. I asked Rocky what he made of so few scars on living pinnipeds in an area frequented by whites. "Well, either few attacks occur," he said, "which I doubt, or most of the attacks are successful. The scars we observed were mostly on small pinnipeds. It may be that the sharks tend to attack the less wily and less agile youngsters and that few of these pups are able to escape after being hit."

The completion of this fifth expedition brought an end to more than two years of joint pioneering work by The Cousteau Society and the South Australian Department of Fisheries. No previous investigators had spent so much time observing great white sharks above and below the water, and no one to our knowledge had ever identified so many individual great whites.

With the completion of this fifth mission, our research team began poring over our data to draw conclusions, and to translate our findings into papers bound for scientific journals and conferences. The totals were impressive:

—— OUR TEAMS HAD OBSERVED SIXTY-SEVEN GREAT WHITE SHARKS.

—— FORTY OF THESE INDIVIDUALS HAD BEEN TAGGED.

—— TWENTY-THREE OF THE TAGGED SHARKS HAD BEEN RE-SIGHTED, FIVE ON TWO OR MORE EXPEDITIONS.

—— NINE GREAT WHITES HAD BEEN TRACKED USING ULTRASONIC EQUIPMENT OVER PERIODS AS LONG AS TWENTY-SEVEN-AND-A-HALF HOURS.

—— THE SIZE OF THE SHARKS OBSERVED RANGED FROM 7.2 FEET TO 18 FEET, WITH AN AVERAGE LENGTH OF 12.1 FEET.

—— COMBINING THE SIGHTINGS AT FIVE LOCATIONS VISITED, WE HAD IDENTIFIED A TOTAL OF 27 FEMALES AND 29 MALES.

Reflecting upon the Cousteau team's experiences, and analyzing our data, Rocky Strong had drawn several conclusions about great white shark behavior.

The first involved the short-term movement of the creatures. From our tracking data, the scientific team could identify three distinctive patterns of movement. Initially, tracked sharks almost always circled downstream of *Alcyone*, apparently crisscrossing over areas where particles of our bait may have settled. This Downstream Circling behavior lasted anywhere from two to twelve hours, and it appeared to be a direct response to chumming. Nevertheless, the scientists found it interesting that the patterns and persistence exhibited by the sharks were so consistent.

After this initial movement, the tracked sharks set out on two different kinds of patterns. The scientists termed one of these patterns Island Patrolling, meaning that the sharks stayed in the vicinity of a nearby island even after the chum had dissipated. *Murf* was such a shark. He remained near Dangerous Reef during the nearly twenty-eight hours we followed him. Perhaps sharks like *Murf* are local residents, at least temporarily, but such a conclusion could only be drawn after much more extensive surveillance.

Antoinette's path away from our vessel represented a third kind of pattern, which we called Inter-Island Cruising. She followed a winding course away from the immediate area, covering nearly 25 miles during 10 hours. As she cruised, she made occasional sorties toward islands encountered along her route. Presumably, she was looking for pinnipeds or other prey as she approached these islands. Such a swimming pattern might also be related to underwater navigational clues, such as seamounts or other structures along the bottom, currents, or even the earth's magnetic field.

Interestingly, during all of these patterns, the average swimming speed of our tracked sharks was just under two miles per hour, the same speed reported during the only other such white shark tracking, which was conducted in the North Atlantic.

Our depth records during the trackings showed that the sharks swam either just below the water surface or along the bottom, where depths averaged about sixty-five feet. When rising or descending, the great whites seemed to spend relatively little time in midwater. Their vertical movements while cruising were gradual and steady, however, and completely unlike the rapid ascents observed when the creatures were rocketing upward toward our surface-borne baits.

Our records generally confirmed that white sharks in South Australia tend to segregate according to gender. Females were most abundant at Dangerous Reef and other inshore islands, while males were found mainly at the Neptunes and other offshore islands. Curiously, this pattern of sexual separation appears to fluctuate over several years for unknown reasons. In the past, according to Rodney Fox and the Taylors, only males were seen at Dangerous Reef during summer months.

We do not know the reasons for this separation. There are many differences between inshore and offshore island habitats, including the water circulation patterns and the bottom topographies. Inshore areas generally tend to be characterized by warmer waters, and it is possible that females seek out such conditions as part of their reproductive strategies. Warmer water would draw less energy from a pregnant mother, and would seem more conducive to the survival of the offspring when born. Also, with fewer adult whites present in these presumably inferior feeding grounds, babies may stand less chance of falling victim to cannibalism by their own kind. Whatever the causes of the segregation—whether environmental or behavioral—they effectively separate members of a species easily capable of swimming the distances between the two areas.

As our expedition began, we had wondered if larger white sharks would spend more time than smaller sharks in the baited area. This did not appear to be the case. Many smaller sharks were quite competitive with the larger sharks in the pursuit of our baits. Since we cannot peer into the creature's brain to know its motivations, it is difficult to draw any conclusions about this. Perhaps some of the smaller white sharks we observed had an especially aggressive demeanor, or perhaps

Barry Bruce studies white shark identification sheets at the chart desk on Alcyone's bridge.

RIGHT:
Detailed shark identification sheets enabled the Cousteau team to recognize sharks that might return to Alcyone. One shark, Rosy, was seen at Dangerous Reef on twenty-four days during a period spanning more than nineteen months and three expeditions.

SPECIES: <u>Carcharodon</u> <u>carcharias</u>

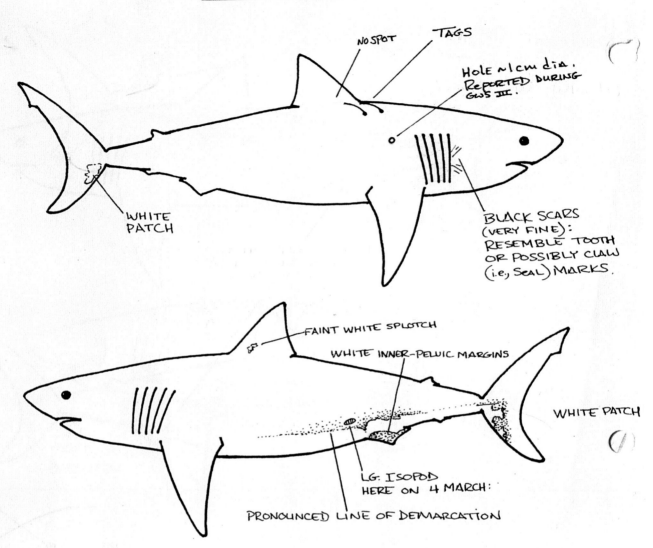

DATE TAGGED: 17 FEB '90   LOCATION: D.R., S.A.

TAG I.D.#: 68155 & 68383   TAG COLOR CODE (SEE LEGEND): 68155=Ⓨ:P
68383=Ⓨ:O:W

SEX: ♀   TOTAL LENGTH: 9'6"   (EST.) or MEAS.
(circle one)

NICKNAME: "ROSY"   TAGGING VESSEL: ALCYONE

REMARKS: NUMEROUS RESIGHTINGS — SEE SIGHTING LOGS
ONLY OBSERVED AT DANGEROUS REEF AS OF 9/90.

Though lacking the eyelid called a nictitating membrane common to some shark species, great whites often rotate their eyes backward at the moment they bump or bite objects. Researchers theorize that this is an adaptation to protect the eye from damage that might be inflicted by a struggling prey. The Cousteau team noticed that when sharks made several runs on bait lines without harm they often discontinued this apparently voluntary eye movement. The dark pores arrayed below the eye are the ampullae of Lorenzini—part of the shark's electrosensory system.

they were simply hungrier and more willing to risk a confrontation with a large shark.

On the other hand, when great whites of different sizes encountered one another head on in the normal course of swimming about, the smaller shark generally gave way. Often, looking suddenly confused, the smaller shark would dash off in a different direction or swing out to give the larger shark unobstructed passage. Sharks that fled often did not return for several minutes. In this regard, we noticed bite marks on several sharks that appeared to have been inflicted by their own species. While the wounds may have come from mating sessions or from a predatory attack, we believed it equally likely that they had resulted from fighting, perhaps for dominance.

As Rocky had emphasized when recounting the events of the last expedition, the sharks rarely tried to take our baits at night. On many occasions, they would remain near our vessel during the hours of darkness, but would not attempt to feed before dawn. Interest in the baits continued through the day and dusk, but diminished quickly with the onset of night.

The tendency toward daytime feeding, along with other observations, gave our scientists the distinct impression that great white sharks are, strongly if not primarily, *visual* predators. Several kinds of white shark behavior seemed to demonstrate excellent vision. We had seen whites rise quickly from depths greater than forty feet to attack targets as small as a drifting, dish-sized clump of sargassum. We saw changes in their body posture, such as fin dips or flinching, that related to movement of baits or divers at considerable distances. Moreover, when chief diver Arrington was replaced in the plastic cylinder by a large tuna, the sharks immediately closed in with heightened interest. And this was despite the fact that the smell of the tuna could hardly have been an attractant in waters already saturated with bait and chum odors.

Finally, our diving team frequently saw the eyes of the great whites fixating on various objects, revealing the white sclera of the eyeball, prior to turning and rushing them from considerable depths and distances. Revealingly, on days when the water was clearest and visiblity enhanced, the sharks made their attacks from deeper and farther away. The notion that great whites could be little more than swimming noses seemed strongly refuted by our experiences.

Reliance upon vision would seem to support our conclusion that great whites are primarily daytime feeders, and the nature of their eyes is in keeping with such behavior. Specialists who have examined great white shark eyeballs describe retinas with abundant cone cells, which are linked to color vision and the ability to see the finer details of an object. While the majority of other shark species studied have eyeballs capable of good vision under low-light conditions, perhaps for night hunting, great whites do not seem similarly equipped, suggesting they make their living for the most part during the daylight hours.

Surely one question above all intrigues the public: why do great white sharks occasionally attack humans? A popular theory is that the sharks mistake swimmers and surfers along the surface for their natural prey—pinnipeds. Indeed, when we provided great whites with the choice between plywood shapes cut into a square or a sea-lion silhouette, they seemed far more likely to inspect the pinniped shape. However, our feeling is that the motivation behind attacks on humans is more complex than a simple case of mistaken identity.

The white sharks we observed would swim after and bite objects of many shapes and sizes, including cardboard boxes, plastic decoys, floating wads of sargassum, and even a cigarette pack that came drifting past. The sharks seemed to be relatively unselective when it came to launching the initial, theoretically investigatory, attack.

To us this suggests that while they seem to rely a great deal on vision, they are unable to determine from a distance if a surface-borne object is going to be palatable. Lacking hands, great white have two principal ways to inspect potential prey: bumping and biting. While bumping may suffice when an object of interest is floating passively, it is of no use in inspecting rapidly moving things, such as sea lions, dolphins, fish, or birds. When highly mobile prey are involved, the logical strategy for a predator without equal agility would be to make a smooth, rapid, surprise approach, to attempt to seize the moving object with the teeth, and then to determine if it was edible.

During these expeditions, our divers spent about 135 hours watching white sharks underwater; the majority of sharks relied heavily on the element of surprise in approaching our baits and other experimental targets, rising quickly from almost directly below the objects, especially when the sharks first arrived at the scene.

Given that great whites seem compelled to launch sneak attacks to bite unknown objects as a way of taste-testing for food, without taking the time to inspect them closely, it is easy to understand why humans are bitten occasionally. Valerie Taylor strongly believes, and many specialists agree, that the risks of being bitten by a great white increase in murky waters. Perhaps, with their vision limited, sharks are even more dependent on an investigatory bite in their search for a meal.

In most cases of a great white attack on a human, however, the victim survives. Perhaps that is because the shark withdraws to let its victim die before consuming it, giving the human an opportunity to reach safety. Or perhaps great white sharks are reluctant to continue feeding on such an unfamiliar prey. Either way, as Rocky quips: "Lucky for us!"

Our original purpose was to help scientists in South Australia determine the size and situation of the great white shark population in the area. Our tagging program and the identification sheets we left behind with local specialists and fishermen should lead eventually to a more accurate estimate of the population than presently exists, as well as to a better understanding of the great white's movement patterns.

Our own conclusion so far is that the area's great whites constitute a relatively local population. Unless new information alters this conclusion, it suggests that there is ample reason for concern about the population's future. A limited community of residential sharks would be far more vulnerable to overexploitation than a population continually repopulated by outsiders. Moreover, under a possible onslaught by fishermen, the separation of the sexes could be a disadvantage for great whites. It appears that females remain in waters most accessible to fishing, so that, for the present at least, they are the most likely to be captured. A few males can mate with numerous females and maintain the stability of a population, but when females become scarce, a population may be unable to survive.

In pondering all of our experiences with the white shark, I was continually struck by the great gulf between what the public imagines the creature to be and what we saw it to be. It is almost universally accepted that sharks of all species are unpredictable and on occasion crazed. Yet time and again, the great whites we watched acted consistently and cautiously. Standing on the deck of *Alcyone*, I often recalled something my father once said: "I do not believe sharks are unpredictable at all. I think we don't understand sharks well enough to predict always what they are going to do next, but I'll bet the shark knows."

I remembered as well a feeling my brother Philippe once expressed about the great white. "If the white shark were really so terrible," he wrote in his book *The Shark*, "it is probable that he would be more widespread, and we would have encountered him more often. Those few we have encountered have fled from us, seemingly terrified at our approach."

Rosy *rockets upward toward a tuna bait at the surface, illustrating the great white's habit of attacking prey in a vertical rush. The Cousteau team witnessed attacks launched from as deep as fifty feet, further evidence that white sharks rely greatly on vision.*

No matter what the truth of the great white shark may be, it will likely be regarded as a monster in the public mind for a long time to come. A few months after *Alcyone* departed South Australian waters, a nineteen-year-old diver was killed by a great white off Aldinga Beach, where Rodney Fox had been attacked twenty-eight years earlier. At about the same time, in separate incidents, two surfers were wounded by great whites not far from an elephant-seal colony south of San Francisco. Despite the scarcity of such attacks before and after these episodes, self-termed shark hunters in both Australia and California called for vigilantelike pursuits to locate and kill the offending sharks. One Australian hunter called for the extermination of the species.

I was reminded of a wave of hysteria that swept South Africa in 1957, after four shark attacks on swimmers south of Durban. The South African Navy dispatched a minesweeper to the area, where they dropped depth charges and hand grenades in a blind assault meant to kill sharks at random and, supposedly, drive them away from the region forever. The explosives succeeded in killing eight sharks, but the countless fish

A series of photos captures the dramatic, and previously undescribed, behavior that occasionally followed a shark's failure to seize a pursued bait. Generally keeping their heads out of the water, the sharks rolled onto their sides, then opened and closed their mouths in a rhythmic gape while swimming slowly along the surface. The biting continued well after the bait was withdrawn, leading observers to believe that the behavior was a sign of frustration after repeated, thwarted attempts to feed.

destroyed incidentally by the explosions attracted even more sharks to the area. So much for shark vigilantism.

Not everyone wants to eliminate the species. To game fishermen it still represents the supreme conquest, and to those who greedily render its jaws into tourist trinkets, it is a steady source of profit. According to Valerie Taylor, the work of catching a great white is not nearly so heroic as one would expect. The creature usually fights gamely for about an hour, she says, then tires and lies quietly along the water. If released, it will swim away, but it may suffer a crash of its metabolism when its breathing diminishes while remaining stationary. Often it can be gaffed and landed rather easily—if hauling in such an immense fish can ever be called easy.

Most people neither hate nor love the great white shark. The plight of our own species, the countless details of daily life, and the fate of wild animals with more endearing characteristics, leave us with little mental energy to invest in worry over, of all things, the most fearsome shark in the sea.

There is no hard evidence that great white shark populations are now in danger. But in South Australia, the most famous domain of white sharks, there are warning signs that cannot be dismissed. Too many people familiar with the life of these waters—Rodney Fox, the Taylors, and dozens of fishermen— testify to the gradual demise of the creature during the past

About twenty percent of the great whites observed by the Cousteau team in South Australia bore white spots on the dorsal fin. Such markings could be genetic markers—indications that sharks in the region form a distinct, relatively isolated population, making them more vulnerable to overexploitation than populations that interbreed with outsiders.

twenty years. Along the coast of New South Wales, where gamefishermen averaged eight great white catches a year during the 1960s and 70s, they averaged only four a year during the 1980s. Meshing net records tell a similarly disconcerting story. In the 1960s, the ratio of other shark species caught in the nets to great whites was 22 to 1. In the 1980s, the ratio was 650 to 1.

Our own observations suggest that fishing—most likely incidental catches by commercial vessels—may be taking a heavy toll on South Australia's great whites. Among the sharks that approached our boats, ten percent were trailing some kind of fishing gear, and thirty percent bore scars that could have come from human contact.

It is possible that the apparent decline of great whites in South Australia may be an environmental phenomenon that causes natural oscillations in the population. Unfortunately, it may take as long as twenty years to know for certain. By that time, given the animal's built-in vulnerability as a slow-growing, long-lived creature that produces relatively few offspring, it could be too late to save the population.

It is our belief that even if great white sharks are not endangered today, they will be ultimately if present trends continue in their exploitation and accidental capture. The loss of such a creature could alter the life of the sea in ways we cannot even imagine.

As an apex predator at the pinnacle of the food web, the great white shark performs vital services that ripple down through the entire pyramid of life below it. By feeding on the less fit members of other marine populations—the old, the weak, the ill, the more feeble young—it culls away individuals of least benefit to the future of their species. Predation by the white shark leads to a situation in which the more fit among its prey share the available resources and in turn produce more fit offspring.

Superpredators like the great white shark—such as orcas and sperm whales—affect waves of adaptation that can cascade all the way down the pyramid of life. If such an influential force over marine life were to disappear the consequences would be enormous and unpredictable. There could be great fluctuations in the number and well-being of species normally preyed upon by white sharks, such as pinnipeds, which could in turn directly affect humans by vastly changing the supply of food we ourselves derive from the sea.

History is replete with examples of what can happen when an apex predator disappears. As shark specialists Samuel Gruber and Charles Manire have pointed out, the removal of the wolf and puma from the American West caused an explosion in the antelope population. Today, these antelope populations must be managed by game wardens at considerable expense to the public.

We must begin to see the white shark not as a potential threat to human swimmers, but as a behind-the-scenes custodian of the life of the sea. It is perhaps within our power to eliminate the white shark in order to make the ocean safer for people. But is it our right? Is it wise?

Only a few weeks after *Alcyone* departed Dangerous Reef for the last time we received word of an important reversal in the age-old perception of the white shark as a worthless killer. South Africa—the same nation that bombed sharks some three decades earlier—had become the first country in the world to protect the great white shark through legislation. Alarmed at the rise in trophy hunting for white-shark jaws, and convinced that the great white plays an extremely important role in the marine ecosystem, the government had outlawed not only the killing of the sharks but the sale of any white-shark product. Said South African Minister of Environment Affairs Louis Pienaar, "The notoriety surrounding the great white shark as a ruthless 'man-eater' is not borne out by the known low and probably incidental human mortalities inflicted by great whites. An indiscriminate and vindictive hunt for great white sharks cannot be tolerated."

To me, the white shark challenges us to raise our environmental consciousness to a new level. If we contemplate protecting this creature, it will not be because it has the harp seal's resemblance to a helpless human infant or the lion cub's similarity to a playful new kitten. It will be because we recognize the vital role in biological diversity and vitality played by a creature without a single endearing trait. It will be because we understand that on a planet of such delicate balances and imperceptible connections we must err on the side of caution. It will be because we realize that it is wiser to tolerate the existence of a potentially dangerous hunter in the sea than to risk unraveling the ocean's sprawling and yet intricate tapestry by removing it.

We may never love the great white shark itself, because it embodies so many ancient and deep-seated human fears—of diabolical beasts, of devils, of giants, of being devoured alive by a hungry, tooth-baring monster. We may always confuse the creature's might with malice, and concentrate in this seldom-seen and little-known animal our elemental dread of the unknown.

We can, however, love certain *aspects* even of the great white shark. We can appreciate it as an organism of proportional beauty, formed into streamlined elegance by time and water and the sculpting effect of evolution. We can admire it as a biological machine of near perfection, equipped with astoundingly sophisticated sensory systems and colossal power, without so much as a bone to gird it.

But beyond that, if the sea itself could love, if the sea were a vast living entity with powers of cognition—in the way it has been portrayed by ancient mythologies rather than by sterile sciences—then the sea itself would love the great white shark. It is an old friend of the sea, roaming it silently, like an antibody to cleanse away life that is wasting or dying, to trim the excesses, to strengthen the breeds.

We may never love the creature itself, but we can love the idea of it, the consequences of its existence, the way it exalts the life of the sea.

Our findings are merely part of the very beginning of deciphering the character and behavior of the great white shark. But each of the forty people who joined us on our expeditions would agree on one simple conclusion. Whatever the white shark may be, it is not a monster. Whatever it inspires in us— dread or wonder—it should not be allowed to vanish forever in the shadows of time.

During the last day of the final mission to Dangerous Reef, while Rocky Strong and Barry Bruce conducted their final experiments and packed up gear, the Ngerin's captain Neal "Chicko" Chigwidden overheard a conversation taking place over the marine radio. A charter-fishing-boat captain was telling an associate on shore that if they found no great whites around English Island, they would sail south to Dangerous Reef. Whenever Ngerin left the area, they planned to occupy the same anchorage and use our chum. Though it is illegal to chum at Dangerous Reef without a permit, there is no law against dropping a hook in the water where authorized chumming such as ours has been carried out.

At 8:30 P.M. on the evening of September 24, the team was ready to take leave of Dangerous Reef and return for the last time to Port Lincoln. Rocky noticed that one of the new sharks,

While searching for white sharks south of Port Lincoln in 1968, Rodney Fox (left), Valerie Taylor (right), and Ron Taylor (who took the photo) came across this dead great white on a commercial fisherman's set line. Apparently unable to extricate itself from the hook, the shark probably suffocated. When the Taylors and Fox discovered the carcass, another great white was engaged in tearing away chunks of meat from the victim's belly. Today, after more than three decades of diving off South Australia, the three veteran shark observers believe similar incidental catches by fishermen are depleting the local great white populations

a fifteen-foot female named *Buttercup*, was still circling through the dissipating cloud of chum at the stern.

Knowing that fishermen would soon arrive in our wake, and that the unsuspecting and somewhat trusting shark could still be in the area, Rocky unpacked his syringe gun, filled it with repellent, and waited along the swimstep until the shark opened her mouth for a bait. He shot a blast of the disagreeable liquid down her throat and she jetted out of sight into the wall of darkness beyond the vessel's stern lamp. When *Buttercup* failed to return for two hours, the team weighed anchor and set out for Port Lincoln.

They knew that beyond the small circle of friends who had participated in these expeditions few would understand the emotions that prompted this small and symbolic final act: the use of shark repellent to save the life of a great white shark.

LEFT ABOVE:
Steve Arrington examines shark jaws in a South Australian curio shop. The unregulated taking of great whites to procure teeth and jaws for the tourist trade may be contributing to what many believe is a severe decrease in the regional population of whites.

LEFT BELOW:
T-shirts in a Port Lincoln, South Australia, gift shop attest to the area's popularity for white-shark fishing and filming. Proponents of conservation argue that short-term profits from shark killing could be exceeded by the economic gains of a tourist industry based on harmless opportunities to observe great white sharks from tour and dive boats.

ABOVE:
A poster entered in a Sydney, Australia, school contest symbolizes the new awareness of sharks as valuable members of the marine ecosystem.

OVERLEAF:
In studying sharks like this one, the Cousteau team hoped that the data gathered would help wildlife managers determine if the great whites of South Australia are in decline. Unfortunately, analysis of fish stocks can take as long as twenty years. In the interim, species like the great white, slow to replicate themselves, could be irretrievably reduced in number, with unpredictable consequences for the equilibrium of life in the sea.

PHOTO CREDITS